The
Sustainability
Scorecard

Urvashi Bhatnagar

and

Paul Anastas

The
Sustainability
Scorecard

How to Implement and Profit from Unexpected Solutions

BK

Berrett–Koehler Publishers, Inc

Berrett-Koehler
Publishers, Inc.
1333 Broadway, Suite 1000
Oakland, CA 94612-1921
Tel: (510) 817-2277
Fax: (510) 817-2278
www.bkconnection.com

ORDERING INFORMATION

Quantity sales. Special discounts are available on quantity purchases by corporations, associations, and others. For details, contact the "Special Sales Department" at the Berrett-Koehler address above.

Individual sales. Berrett-Koehler publications are available through most bookstores. They can also be ordered directly from Berrett-Koehler: Tel: (800) 929-2929; Fax: (802) 864-7626; www.bkconnection.com.

Orders for college textbook / course adoption use. Please contact Berrett-Koehler: Tel: (800) 929-2929; Fax: (802) 864-7626.

Distributed to the US trade and internationally by Penguin Random House Publisher Services.

Berrett-Koehler and the BK logo are registered trademarks of Berrett-Koehler Publishers, Inc.

Printed in the United States of America

Berrett-Koehler books are printed on long-lasting acid-free paper. When it is available, we choose paper that has been manufactured by environmentally responsible processes. These may include using trees grown in sustainable forests, incorporating recycled paper, minimizing chlorine in bleaching, or recycling the energy produced at the paper mill.

Library of Congress Cataloging-in-Publication Data
Names: Bhatnagar, Urvashi, author. | Anastas, Paul T., 1962- author.
Title: The sustainability scorecard : how to implement and profit from unexpected solutions / Urvashi Bhatnagar and Paul Anastas.
Description: First Edition. | Oakland, CA : Berrett-Koehler Publishers, [2022] | Includes bibliographical references and index.
Identifiers: LCCN 2021050955 (print) | LCCN 2021050956 (ebook) | ISBN 9781523093786 (hardcover) | ISBN 9781523093793 (pdf) | ISBN 9781523093809 (epub)
Subjects: LCSH: Sustainable development—Management. | Business Logistics—Environmental aspects. | Management—Technological innovations.
Classification: LCC HD75.6 .B5143 2022 (print) | LCC HD75.6 (ebook) | DDC 658.4/08—dc23/eng/20211213
LC record available at https://lccn.loc.gov/2021050955
LC ebook record available at https://lccn.loc.gov/2021050956

First Edition

27 26 25 24 23 22   10 9 8 7 6 5 4 3 2 1

Book producer: Susan Geraghty
Cover designer: Nita Ybarra
Interior design: Lewelin Polanco

To all the scientists, teachers, businesspeople, inventors, industrialists, investors, communicators, financers, activists, managers, and public servants around the globe who are advancing green chemistry for the goal of a better world.

—P.A.

To the future generations of leaders in every field who will find creative ways to redefine, reengineer, and resolve humanity's most pressing economic issues to create a new reality.

—U.B.

Contents

Foreword

These next few decades, a length of time that spans only a single human's typical career from start to finish, will be some of the most transformative in human history. Transformative in the sense that nearly everything we do needs to change.

When we examine the big things we do—electricity, transportation, food, all the stuff that we consume, and all the activities that we enjoy—essentially none of it is currently sustainable. What is worse, much of it causes external damage to the climate and the natural world that our descendants will hate us for. There is mounting evidence that we are precipitating the sixth great mass extinction in our planet's history. This is not good.

To many people, the entire concept of sustainable products and systems sounds like some eco-utopian fuzzy-headed vision promoted by college students. In truth, sustainability is just common sense. Herbert Stein, an economist, has a quote that I've always liked, "If something cannot go on forever, it will stop." Although he was referring to certain financial imbalances, the same is true for all endeavors.

When a company provides products or services that are not sustainably sourced, by definition that means its products or services are unsustainable and will eventually stop. This is in addition to any external environmental damage the product's production or use might be responsible for, whose costs generally fall on someone else.

From a purely capitalist standpoint, it is important for investors and management to recognize that their company's products or services will stop being viable even if customers still want to buy them. This isn't an ESG threat but simply a fact. If a product depends on processes and inputs that are not sustainable, it will stop being a viable product as shortages or input prices make it unsuccessful in the marketplace. That isn't fuzzy-headed "green" thinking, but a sign of the need for very clear, proactive management.

In the recent past, a large US cereal company proclaimed its green credentials on every cereal box, stating in large, bold letters: "We have committed to sustainably source 100% of our cereal boxes by 2020." Clearly people in the supply chain of this large company were working hard on sourcing boxes, and it was comforting to know that the future of cereal boxes would be secure. However, the future of what is inside the cereal boxes is far less certain. I assume that the inputs that make the cereal are not sustainably managed, and those farms are mining water or topsoil or fertilizer or some other resource in a way that will eventually cause their fields to fail. If that weren't the case, I'm sure it would be also in large letters on the soon-to-be sustainable box. The farms won't fail this quarter, or probably this decade, but maybe in two decades? Three? I am not sure, but if I were on their board of directors, or held their stock, I certainly would want to know.

Of course, such issues pertain not just to cereal but to just about all the goods and services that we now consume. We need to make millions of supply and production changes, from initial design, sourcing of resources, through to final product delivery, but then back again so that those embodied resources can be reprocessed into new things. We need to build a truly circular economy.

There are many people who argue that a better way is to "de-grow," to go back to simpler lifestyles from earlier times and consume far less. There are many real and virtual communities dedicated to this simpler, less resource-intensive lifestyle, living more holistically, which is wonderful. Subjectively, much of what our society produces seems to be a waste of time and resources and can present financial strain on people who "need" those things.

But a truly utopian society allows everyone to reach their potential and have a reasonable shot to fulfill their hopes and dreams. For some people, that appears to require long chains of purple plastic unicorns that light up in synchronized ways to music. My personal happiness does not depend on plastic unicorns, but probably on other things many people find equally absurd. Our future should not be one of proscribed grand austerity, but rather one making sure that the plastic used to make unicorns contains carbon from the present and is completely biodegradable, or at a minimum will be recycled back into virgin material for the next mythical creature. That the copper and other mined elements will be recaptured to make future products that delight the user. Doing this requires changes in product design, use of new materials, and better recycling systems. But none of that is fantasy or science fiction, just work, and we are pretty good at such things as a society if we care about it.

And this represents an enormous opportunity for entrepreneurs and companies. We need to literally reinvent the entire world economy over these next few decades—not only moving into a sustainable low-carbon-emissions world but also providing for an additional several billion people while increasing the standard of living of billions of others who are already with us. It feels like a heavy lift, but we don't have a choice. The ghost of Stein tells us that "it will stop" if we don't fix it.

Toward the end of this book, the authors profile a few of the thousands of new technologies that clever entrepreneurs are pursuing to this end. These efforts are taking place all over the world and will challenge many of the large corporations (and perhaps governments) that dominate the world marketplace. Many of them will fail, but collectively we will learn what works and change the world. Entrenched systems and globe-spanning companies may appear impossible to dislodge, but consider that none of the top-ten most valuable companies today were on that list in 1990. Many didn't even exist in 1990. Big changes can happen within only a few decades, and when there is a crisis like the one we just encountered with COVID-19, we now know big change can be much faster than that.

Progress is not inevitable. We literally will the future into existence through our small individual actions. There have been many times in our collective history when things did not get better for centuries. We don't have that luxury of time now. Personally, I want a future of sustainable abundance that lets us explore the world, have fantastic experiences, and provide a full life for all. I hope that everyone who reads this book will be inspired to build a better sustainable future, whatever their particular dreams are.

—MARC TARPENNING,
COFOUNDER, TESLA INC.

Doing Better Things Better

> It ain't what we know that gets us in trouble, it's what we know for sure that just ain't so.
>
> —*Mark Twain*

I magine, for a moment, a car. Any color you like, midrange, any brand. Do you have it? It runs well and does the job, taking you from home to work, with a detour to the gym in the evening before you return home. You pass your state and emissions inspections without any trouble, and you're not really thinking of upgrading anytime soon. It gives you about 27 miles per gallon—the average mpg in 2020—just 6 mpg higher than the Model T released over a hundred years ago.[1]

Henry Ford introduced the Model T, the gas-powered disruptor to the transportation industry, way back in 1908.[2] It was a brilliant innovation for its time, launching the automobile industry as we know it. Before 1908, cars were considered a luxury item, custom designed for wealthy individuals.[3] There were fewer than two hundred thousand cars on US roads, and they were priced at approximately $18,000 in today's dollars.[4] Ford's assembly-line production model significantly reduced the cost of production and spurred systems engineers to create further efficiencies.[5] Efficiencies drove scale and mass production, and cars soon permeated every price segment in society. By 1914, Ford was producing approximately three hundred thousand cars annually, surpassing the cumulative production of every other car manufacturer in the market. Eventually, ordinary individuals across America were driving cars to work.[6]

The impact of the Model T cannot be understated. It is the Model T, in fact, that is credited with spurring US government investment in infrastructure and roadways. Henry Ford did not just innovate the product and process; he transformed the auto industry. At a time when cars were not expected to have any significant impact on the economy at all, he democratized access to transportation and significantly influenced the American economy.[7] The automobile industry enabled the launch of many other industries, enabled robust capital markets, and furthered rigorous research into competitive strategy and operations.[8]

Yet in over a century we've improved fuel efficiency by a measly six miles per gallon.

Now consider the story of Okjokull (Ok, pronounced "awk"), the first-ever glacier to die at the hands of climate change. Ok covered 10 percent of one of Iceland's eight islands, the ice enmeshed into the natural landscape and into the lives of all who lived there. Because of global warming, the glacier lost so much ice that what remained melted where it sat.

In August 2019, Iceland held a funeral for Ok with poem recitals, remembrance speeches, and even an orbit by NASA satellites, the first-ever funeral by orbit for a nonhuman being. Citizens, scientists, and politicians all gathered to pay their respects. A plaque now commemorates the place where the ice once lay, with crusty earth and puddles of water sporadically breaking the landscape.

Ok's death had and continues to have devastating implications for Iceland—from water resources to infrastructural issues and even to the rising of land due to a lighter load of ice on its surface. It was a bleak sign for a country named after its vast coverage of ice and that is home to more than four hundred glaciers. It will lose them all in the next two hundred years. Iceland is certainly not "OK."

As Icelandic writer and environmental activist Andri Snær, who was integral to the organization of the funeral ceremony, wrote, "Our existence is going against future generations. That's an unbearable, existential dilemma. We're sacrificing the lives of the next generation for our own. Not even for survival but for comfort, which is probably the most absolute ethical situation that any generation has found itself in."[9]

Central to this sad tale is the energy crisis globally and, locally, Iceland's energy harnessing practices. The Environmental Agency of Iceland reported an approximate 85 percent increase in greenhouse gas (GHG) emissions from the island from 1990 to the present day.[10] Of the entire GHG emissions produced by the country, heavy industry emissions constitute 48 percent of the total—even though these heavy industrial facilities run on renewable energy sources such as hydroelectric and thermal power![11] Large amounts of carbon dioxide are still released as a part of the process of smelting aluminum and processing silicon metals for steel manufacturing.

The Icelandic government has set goals for achieving climate neutrality; however, those goals are ambitious considering that renewable inputs are already the source for the industrial complex.

The country offers free public transportation between locations on "gray days" when pollution levels are high, and drivers are encouraged to use mass transit to reduce the pollution on heavy-smog days. However, more action is needed, and any strategy implemented by Iceland will have to tackle existing methods for processing aluminum and steel. Had the entire economic-industrial complex been evaluated when the hydroelectric and thermal power project was considered, and if environmental and social factors were included in the assessment, maybe Ok would still be alive.

We've Been Doing Things Wrong for So Long; Our Future Is Full of Opportunities

The reason that today is different from one hundred years ago is that people designed it to be different. Henry Ford invented the modern-day assembly line and Model T to scale the automobile industry. Iceland's heavy industry designed steel-manufacturing processes to support and grow the country's economy. Globally, the brightest minds and most disruptive firms have placed a relentless focus on efficiency, growth, and innovation, but what they are really doing is designing the future and our present. And, as the examples here show, there are critical vulnerabilities in the current design, and we have a long way to go in designing a sustainable future.

Here are a just a few examples of the design flaws in traditional products and processes:

- The amount of waste generated to make a semiconductor microchip is over 100,000 times the weight of the chip.[12]
- One ton of paper utilizes 98 tons of various material inputs.[13]
- Of all materials used in the creation of everyday products, 95 percent end up as waste.[14]
- Hospitals create 12 percent of the acid rain in the United States, 10% of the smog, and 200,000 newborn premature deaths by way of their GHG emissions.[15]
- We would require the natural resources of five additional Earths for the global population to live as comfortably as the average American.[16]

We've never heard of anyone asking for an x-ray with a small amount of climate change on the side. However, by continuing to passively accept the traditional design constructs we live in, that's precisely what we're doing.

Economist Herbert Simon once said, "An efficient individual is someone that attempts rationally to maximize the attainment of certain ends with the use of scarce means." By that definition, our everyday lives are littered with examples of "efficiency gone awry"—for example, solar/photovoltaic cells, pesticides, gold mining, fracking, supply-chain redundancies, and industrial farming.

When most of the products we use today were first conceived, in many cases over one hundred years ago, we had little knowledge of what their environmental impact would be. The Industrial Revolution of the late 1800s occurred under the assumption that natural resources were abundant and infinite. At the same time, advances in medical technology increased human life spans and the number of people on the planet. This meant that humans could conduct economic activity at a rapid pace and leverage those resources for a longer span of time per person. The rapid increase in industrial activity set into motion poorly designed business systems and an entire age of efficiency gone awry. We had little appreciation back then for the toxic health effects that could result from not only the products we used but also the by-products of their manufacture. And as time went on, these systems, these unsustainably designed ways of doing things, were normalized and, just like tribal wisdom, passed down through generations without disruption or question.

Today, our interconnected and global supply chains are more advanced than ever, with machine learning models providing firms with predictive analytics on supply and demand. However, natural resources are getting scarcer and more expensive. Firms now face the threat of increased costs of doing business and competition for the same resources that were abundant during the Industrial Revolution. Meanwhile, global supply chains face disruption with the rise of political unrest due to this competition for resources as well as the increased frequency of extreme weather. With embedded capital in existing systems and leading firms ill equipped to navigate these environmental threats, we realize now that a few things are for certain:

To continue to accept these realities is *absurdity*.

To not do anything about them is *obscenity*.

To not profit from the unexpected solutions that sustainability offers would be *humankind's greatest missed opportunity*.

The Sustainability Scorecard and Its Unexpected Solutions

It may feel as though we're stuck somewhere between *absurdity* and *obscenity*, but as far as solutions go—that is, getting us as far away from *missed opportunity* as possible—problems can't be solved at the same level that created them. We will have to think differently if we want to design a better future.

Before plunging into design solutions for the future, it helps to understand what we're designing for. What do we want the next fifty to one hundred years to look like? This book has been written from a very specific point of view, one based on a very precise sustainable *and* profitable design for the future of all human economic activity.

The status quo tells us that sustainability comes at the price of compromising quality or efficacy, ultimately costing more for a poorer experience. In our vision for the future, sustainably designed products actually perform *better* than unsustainable ones, with increased efficiency and quality. And this higher performance of the product depends on sustainability and profitability walking hand in hand. The way we see it, "making green out of green" is the only way forward. We must redesign our products and processes to be environmentally benign and nontoxic. Anything less is neither efficient nor profitable over the long term. In other words, it's unsustainable—financially and otherwise.

To design this future, we must address the building blocks of our processes at every level. Whether it is our continued reliance on rare-earth metals, on petrochemicals for fuel in vehicles, or on the production of plastics, we need to create circular and interdisciplinary solutions to ensure that we are designing for a sustainable and profitable future.

In other words, economic activity of every kind must be designed to encompass what we refer to as the Four Principles for Managing and Scaling Sustainability:

1. Waste prevention
2. Maximizing efficiency and performance
3. Renewable inputs
4. Safe degradation

These principles act as design constraints, elements that must be embedded in the product or process—and that is what yields unexpected solutions, sometimes even breakthrough innovations, such as carbon-negative vodka. In fact, the most compelling argument for including sustainability in an enterprise-wide corporate strategy might just be capitalizing on the unexpected value that traditional business practices leave on the table. When these sustainability-related constraints are not present—as was the case a hundred years ago—then the design process yields completely different results (i.e., the traditional, unsustainable products we have today).

Herbert Stein observed in his economic analysis of GDP that "if something cannot go on forever, it stops." In determining what we can do to counter the economic shocks from climate change, this should be our mindset: sustainability is the only solution, the only one that will keep things going. Of course, the challenge remains: How can businesses operate with cost consciousness while abiding by the four sustainability management principles? In other words, how can they align sustainable design with their other strategic business priorities? To answer this important question, we developed the Sustainability Scorecard, which measures progress toward long-term sustainability *and* profitability.

The key metrics of the Sustainability Scorecard incorporate characteristics of science and technology in combination with the social, financial, environmental, and governance metrics we measure today. They serve as progress indicators toward a global economy that is renewable rather than depleting, healthful rather than toxic, and circular rather than linear.

The Sustainability Scorecard—this book and the metrics—is about how to do better things (i.e., sustainability) better (i.e., profitably). In this book, we explore sustainable product design and scaling green innovations profitably through reducing operating costs, expanding market share, creating new service lines, and—our main focus area—transforming supply-chain and sourcing models to drive the most consistent and highest long-term value. We will show you not only that it can be done but that it's already being done by leading-edge firms all over the world. Our sustainable and profitable vision for the world is already coming to fruition with innovative start-ups using the Sustainability Scorecard to come up with unexpected solutions to some of our most pressing environmental problems:

- The creation of the first-ever carbon-negative vodka—its production removes more carbon dioxide from the environment than it consumes
- The development of artificial photosynthesis to produce ammonia more efficiently, not only for use as fertilizer but also in the creation of sustainable fuel cells
- The use of worms to remove contaminants from wastewater, resulting in a 91% reduction in GHG emissions in local wastewater treatment facilities

What's more, we will explore the green chemistry and sustainability innovations of the future that we believe will disrupt key industries and drive the economy over the next fifty to one hundred years. Through our deep dive into these unexpected products and processes, we will show you how you can use our repeatable, data-driven framework to integrate sustainability into your overall corporate strategy—and to profit from it.

There are several scorecards out there that approach climate change economics and business decision-making; however, none of them are driven by science. The Sustainability Scorecard is the first scientifically rooted, data-driven methodology for strategic, sustainable transformation. It guides organizations in designing a future that is healthful, circular (i.e., restorative and replenishing by design), *and* effective in leveraging climate economics—what we see as the greatest business opportunity of our times.

Who We Are and Our Why

Paul Anastas and Urvashi Bhatnagar here. Here's a bit about us and why scaling sustainability and the Sustainability Scorecard are so important to us.

URVASHI

I am a healthcare professional and have held various leadership positions in a variety of roles within healthcare. My interest in environmental sustainability was an offshoot of my early career focus in India in physical medicine and rehabilitation and public health. I began my career as a physical therapist intern at St. Stephen's Hospital in Tis Hazari, New Delhi, home to the Physical Medicine and Rehab unit led by Dr. Matthew Varghese. Dr. Varghese, an orthopedic surgeon, is well known for his impact and leadership in reconstructive surgery and rehabilitation of polio and post-polio syndrome, even drawing mention from Bill Gates in his blog "Gates Notes."[17] I learned from him about social and environmental determinants of health, and his work in the field of health equity had a lasting impact on my professional and personal development. During that internship, the interaction between our natural environment and human health became clear to me, and I dedicated my career to improving healthcare access and delivery to the communities that require it the most. While pursuing my doctor of physical therapy degree from Boston University, I designed and led community health programs in my clinical practice as a program director in northern Virginia and expanded service-line offerings to impact total patient wellness in my practice. I went on to design and lead complex, integrated system transformations in almost every aspect of the healthcare system and have designed programs at the 50,000-foot level leveraging cutting-edge science and analytics to effect change at the ground level. I am particularly passionate about scaling access and delivery of high-quality care to the communities that require it the most.

While I was working on my MBA at Yale School of Management, I happened to attend a talk by Paul at the National Arboretum in Washington, DC. He discussed the power and importance of designing for the future and the role of management systems that support innovation and scaling; subsequent to the lecture, I changed my academic focus area from healthcare to sustainability.

Currently, there exists an abject lack of focus on the role that circular economies and inherently sustainable products play in human health within the healthcare industry, and more leadership is required within healthcare to evolve current practices in a manner that is holistically beneficial for patients. In essence, leaders today are designing the care delivery of the future, and I believe that the principles outlined in this book will support the overall transformation that our industry requires to enable patients to thrive fifty to one hundred years into the future.

What we are currently experiencing in healthcare in the digital age—the collapse of silos within care delivery all the way from a patient's first interaction with the healthcare ecosystem to the services engaged until final recovery—are in essence taking us toward the larger goal of sustainability and developing closed-loop systems. So the accelerated adoption of digital and advanced analytics platforms in direct patient care, an increased focus on inequity and inequality, and efforts to increase transparency in the health system are in reality all solutions to healthcare sustainability issues. At a macro level, this is the market executing shifts along the curvilinear relationship between social responsibility and financial performance. I believe it is my and my colleagues' responsibility to design care delivery models with this forward-looking approach for future generations through the development of closed-loop systems and innovative financing solutions, and through taking a leading position embedding the triple-bottom-line approach in all areas of healthcare.

Every firm in the economy works in tandem with the communities it serves, and interacts with every other industry to create social, financial, and environmental impacts. This means that every firm has a business case to impact the health, wellness, and future survival of its stakeholders and the world at large.

I believe that social and environmental determinants of health and the key sustainability metrics identified by the United Nations, also known as the United Nations Sustainable Development Goals, are one and the same except in terms of scale. Consequently, evaluating and improving these metrics are key not only to the long-term future of our planet but also to improving the long-term wellness of our global communities. The externalities of our economic activities have a direct impact on the quality of our living environment and therefore on human health.

PAUL

I am, first and foremost, a beakers-and-flask chemist, and received my BA and MA in chemistry from the University of Massachusetts in Boston and a PhD from Brandeis University. I began my career at the EPA, where I was able to launch the first official research program into the field of green chemistry. I founded the Green Chemistry Institute in 1997 at the American

Chemical Society and served at the White House Office of Science and Technology Policy from 1999 to 2004. I returned to the EPA in 2009 as the assistant administrator for the Office of Research and Development and as the science advisor. I currently serve as the director of Yale University's Center for Green Chemistry and Green Engineering, and hold multiple appointments at Yale University and other visiting lectureship roles, fellowships, and honorary doctorates. I have cofounded several firms to drive new chemistry and bring entirely new products into the market, accelerating the process of innovation in driving products from research labs to commercial utilization, and have worked with leading global organizations to advance their sustainability practices.

My lifelong interest and activism in environmental science began when I was a child growing up in Quincy, Massachusetts, a small town outside Boston. My home overlooked a beautiful wetland, teeming with wildlife and flora unique to the microclimate of the area. Over the course of my childhood, this wetland was bulldozed to make way for office space and shopping centers. I was furious at the time and could not understand how such an activity could be sanctioned on the clearly abundant wetland. At around the same time, the EPA, which had just been founded by Richard Nixon, launched an essay contest to promote science and technology. At the age of eight, I won the contest and received recognition from Nixon—an honor that to this day adorns my office at the Yale School of the Environment in New Haven, Connecticut.

At the Institute for Green Chemistry, my partner John Warner and I developed the Twelve Principles of Green Chemistry. They provide the design constraints for developing and scaling inherently sustainable products and processes. These twelve principles, and their extrapolation into the sustainability management principles in this book, are the result of countless peer-reviewed studies. Their application has enabled market-shaping innovators and organizations to produce a curvilinear relationship between business, environment, society, and finances.[18] This means that as the environmental and social performance of the firm improves, the financial performance of the firm increases as well.

Our Journey

The sustainability and management concepts discussed in this book are an extension of Paul's inspiring talk at the National Arboretum. Our journey over the few years following the inspiring discussion at the National Arboretum spanned collaboration in furthering the role of green chemistry as a design element for innovation-leading organizations. In addition, we also advised leaders in all industries with thought leadership related to supply-chain and management frameworks that address the human health impacts of economic activities. Urvashi was also fortunate enough to participate in workshops with leading healthcare researchers and professionals looking to apply environmental and social good factors to healthcare, and to attend industry events and conferences in the sustainability space. The more she explored the sustainability arena, the more surprised she became by the lack of focus on environmental and human health and wellness. This disconnect between individuals' deeply personal wellness goals and our passive acceptance of the negative impacts of our economic activities was appalling to us both. That is why we set out to discover how the Twelve Principles of Green Chemistry (in collaboration with Paul's and Julie Zimmerman's pathbreaking work in the development of the Twelve Principles of Green Engineering) could address the critical issues that affect human health and wellness.

We believe that in our economy today, every firm has a business case to directly impact the health and sustainability of the communities it serves.

The question we strive to answer in this book is *How?*

> How should sustainability be incorporated into corporate strategy?
>
> How should sustainable processes and products be designed?
>
> How should supply chains be transformed?
>
> How should management efforts be tracked?
>
> How should potential solutions be evaluated to understand their impact?
>
> Which actions will truly progress the goals of business and society?

It became clear to us that executives need a framework to help them evaluate which solutions will result in the greatest impact to their bottom line as well as to their environmental and social goals. That's why we developed the Sustainability Scorecard.

Although most industries today track key performance indicators (KPIs) related to carbon and their overall sustainability goals, these are usually based on a risk management assessment, and, therefore, the focus is risk mitigation. With the Sustainability Scorecard, we are providing a path for firms to think much bigger and much more strategically about how they can leverage sustainability to transform their business and long-term trajectory—to design unexpected solutions that lead to a better future for themselves and for the world.

How to Use This Book

Sustainable practices and closed-loop solutions at large corporations have the power to create wide-scale, diversified impact—when they are embedded into the strategy and innovation arms of organizations. For companies to truly and meaningfully take advantage of the opportunity that sustainability has to offer, we outline a number of product design strategies and innovation-related activities in this book.

First in this book, we walk you through the lies about sustainability that the status quo implicitly and explicitly tells us, and how we know they're wrong. No, firms don't use toxic materials just because they are much cheaper than harmless ones, and no, green products don't need to cost more for a poorer experience. This is simply the flawed thinking that has led to the flawed design of our present. In the first chapter, we provide the evidence to inform you and your firm's improved thinking so that you can design a better future. In chapter 2, we dive deep into the four guiding principles of sustainability management that every C-suite executive should use to inform the sustainability strategy for their organization. In chapter 3, we introduce the most exciting and practical part: the Sustainability Scorecard.

The Sustainability Scorecard shows how sustainable design can align the strategic priorities of organizations with their overall footprint. It provides key metrics that firms can use to track their journey toward increasing sustainability in their processes and products.

We acknowledge here that we understand that the sustainability space is scorecard rich. Depending on organizational priorities, there are numerous ones to choose from. With several online tools, users can customize their organizational scorecard depending on firm size, location, and market positioning (for example, a product or service firm). To better understand the pain points and gaps in existing scorecards in the market, we attended a presentation by sustainability leader Bob Willard, hosted by the Sustainable Purchasing Leadership Council. Bob has spent over three decades in senior leadership at IBM and now, by way of his firm Sustainability Advantage, has created, developed, and refined a very useful tool to further organizational sustainability for procurement professionals and has conducted an in-depth analysis of existing scorecards. He mentions that most tools existing today focus on three main categories of indicators:

- Environmental metrics: wherein materiality and material-related emissions are tracked
- Employee-related metrics: wherein wages and other social factors are tracked
- Community impact: wherein ethics, donations, lobbying activities, and factors related to business ethics are tracked

The gaps in current tools today related to supply-chain transparency, understanding the effect of renewables not only on emissions but on product design and end of life, and the factoring in of product performance in a triple-bottom-line fashion demonstrate exactly where our scorecard fits in. As you will see in just a few pages, we track organizational activities under broad, scientific categories. These categories differentiate our scorecard from others, right at the outset. We focus on

- Waste prevention (where we recommend a proactive assessment of future waste, conducted in the design phase)
- Maximizing efficiency and performance (with an expanded definition of performance whereby social and environmental considerations are tracked)
- Renewable resources (where we focus on supply-chain inputs and, thereby, inherited inputs)
- Safe degradation (where we attempt to design a safe and benign afterlife for products and processes)

This scorecard is intended to be proactive. So, by way of its design, it enables firms not only to understand existing gaps but to address supply-chain inputs and change procurement strategies to address material loops, include a triple-bottom-line view of product performance, embed product stewardship into end-of-life considerations, and take a proactive approach to renewable inputs.

The beauty of the Sustainability Scorecard is that it offers nonreductive, strategic KPIs that align with the four sustainability management principles and that can guide firms along their unique sustainability journeys. But we didn't design this framework to be rigid—as technology evolves, innovations occur, and our world changes, our KPIs will serve as well-researched suggestions to spark conversation and ideation to find the metrics that are most meaningful for individual firms. The Sustainability Scorecard is a high-level guide, not a one-size-fits-all solution for each firm in each industry.

In chapter 4, we walk you through how to use the Sustainability Scorecard to assess where your firm is on your sustainability journey—the Initiate, Develop, or Mature stage—and discuss the different strategic goals and timelines that will move you from taking a risk-based approach to sustainability to leveraging it as a strategic differentiator. We use the example of global health technology giant Philips to show how mature-stage firms can employ enterprise-wide operational transformation to achieve their climate goals.

We will preview our four-part scorecard here and then dive into the details later in this book.

The sustainability scorecard has four main sections that are derived from the four principles of sustainability management. Within each section we describe certain key performance indicators. As we describe later in this book, this scorecard is intended to be flexible and customizable for firms in each industry. While many assessment tools currently exist in the market, it is intended to provide a high-level view of all the firm's sustainability to help executives increase the footprint of "green" products and processes in their firms. Let's dive in!

SUSTAINABILITY SCORECARD
PART 1: WASTE PREVENTION

KPI	SUB-METRIC	PRODUCT/ PROCESS 1	UNEXPECTED SOLUTION:	RATING
Economy of waste	Atom economy (in g/mol, percentage)			
	E-factor			
	Packaging: percentage of readily recyclable material			
Economy of space	Number of units per square foot of product			
	Number of units transported per vehicle			
Process intensification	Productivity/ size ratio			
	Productivity/ weight ratio			

PART 2: MAXIMIZING EFFICIENCY AND PERFORMANCE

KPI	SUB-METRIC	PRODUCT/ PROCESS 1	PRODUCT/ PROCESS 2 (UNEXPECTED SOLUTION)	RATING
Material efficiency	Mass of recycled material/total mass Mass of renewable material/total mass			
Environmental health metrics	Global warming potential (in kg CO_2 equivalent)			
	Acidification potential (in kg CO_2 equivalent)			
	Eutrophication potential (in kg N equivalent)			
	Smog formation potential (in kg O emissions)			

(continued)

PART 2: MAXIMIZING EFFICIENCY AND PERFORMANCE (continued)

KPI	SUB-METRIC	PRODUCT/ PROCESS 1	PRODUCT/ PROCESS 2 (UNEXPECTED SOLUTION)	RATING
Human health metrics	Number of restricted chemicals according to EU and US guidelines			
	Percentage of chemicals linked to high acuity, disease, and procedural complexity (i.e., high-cost patients)			
	Percentage of chemicals linked to high acuity, disease, and procedural complexity (i.e., moderately high-cost patients)			
	Percentage of chemicals with robust data sources on assessment of health impacts			

PART 3: RENEWABLE RESOURCES

KPI	SUB-METRIC	PRODUCT/ PROCESS 1 BEFORE SUSTAINABILITY TRANSFORMATION	PRODUCT/ PROCESS 2 (UNEXPECTED SOLUTION)	RATING
Renewable carbon-free energy inputs	Percentage of renewable carbon (a measure of all carbon sources that avoid fossil fuel sources) Percentage of carbon-negative sources (percentage of sources of product input that remove more carbon than they produce)			
Waste energy utilization				
Renewable feedstocks	Percentage of total inputs that are derived from renewable resources			

PART 4: SAFE DEGRADATION

KPI	SUB-METRIC	PRODUCT/ PROCESS 1 BEFORE SUSTAINABILITY TRANSFORMATION	PRODUCT/ PROCESS 2 (UNEXPECTED SOLUTION)	R A T I N G
Persistence (a measure of transgenerational design)	Percentage of "forever chemicals" in final product			
Bioaccumulation	Bioaccumulation factor			
Exposure	Induction period and duration of product life			
	Latent period and duration of product life			

Each part of this scorecard has its own legend; we will describe this in much more detail in a separate chapter.

When sustainability becomes part of a firm's overall growth strategy, that's when the magic happens. In the future that we hope to design, sustainability will be a strategic differentiator for all firms and industries, not just a risk management initiative where we check off boxes and do the bare minimum. That's why in chapter 5 we address the first, fundamental step in developing sustainable solutions: design. By designing and redesigning from the bottom up with sustainability as a key focus, firms open themselves up to unexpected solutions, to leapfrog innovations, and to valuable new products and processes that simply don't occur when the low bar is risk avoidance. We offer a simple three-step process to design new and innovative products and processes that align with the sustainability management principles and that firms can track using the Sustainability Scorecard.

We understand that innovation in large firms looks different from that in more nimble start-ups that are able to pivot their strategies and products based on market demand and to more immediately capture value. And although large firms have several advantages for scaling innovation, they face the challenge of embedded capital (financial and human) in established processes. That's why we devote chapter 6 to the ways in which larger organizations can kick-start their sustainability journeys, including launching pilot programs and using drop-in replacements, before scaling across service lines using the Sustainability Scorecard metrics.

For smaller firms, start-ups, and investors looking for their next big bets, in chapter 7 we identify the emerging sustainable technologies that we expect to be commercialized and scaled in the next fifty to one hundred years. Firms and investors can leverage the Sustainability Scorecard to assess these technologies, including whether the new solution prevents waste, is maximally efficient and performative, uses renewable inputs, and degrades safely, in order to understand its true value proposition.

Our hope in this book is to persuade you not only of the viability but also of the profitability and unexpected value of sustainable "farm-to-table" supply chains. We believe that maximizing sustainability at every phase of your product's or processes' life cycle will be the ultimate differentiator going forward, and the Sustainability Scorecard is your path to getting there strategically and profitably. In chapter 8, we present case studies of two firms—Gundersen Health Systems and Coastwide Laboratories—that embedded sustainable practices throughout their supply chains. We highlight their bold yet replicable steps that we can all learn from. They are shining beacons for how we all can and must take a forward-facing approach to integrating sustainability into corporate strategy.

Our Promise to You

In this book, we present you with the details for how to assess, implement, and scale unexpected solutions in an effort to maximize your financial, environmental, and social bottom lines.

We identify inherently sustainable solutions that actually move the needle with respect to financial, environmental, and social factors. We provide a framework for your firm to identify truly innovative, inherently sustainable products as opposed to "less bad" products and processes that may not provide the exponential value that breakthrough products can.

We explore how to design sustainable products and processes that will create value fifty to one hundred years into the future. And, just as important, we show how you can use the scorecard to measure and track the progress of processes and products toward increasingly greater sustainability. Near the end of the book, we also provide a list of recommended reading that can help you dive into the scientific research and data that inform our framework. Should you be so inclined to read further about the latest green chemistry and green engineering research, we have curated a list of initial reading material for you to explore as well as a reference to the Center for Green Chemistry and Green Engineering at Yale University—a think tank and research and development lab led by Paul Anastas that partners with leading organizations globally to develop and commercialize breakthrough products and processes. Lastly, but certainly not the least, we guide you through the process of creating your own Sustainability Scorecard metrics that align with your company's unique strategic priorities.

The Sustainability Scorecard was written for operations and strategy executives who love the idea and value proposition of sustainability, but don't feel that they have the bandwidth to implement and scale these changes at their firms. You do—if you take things one step at a time. This is how the Sustainability Scorecard solves one of the biggest challenges for firms: how to continue operating with cost consciousness while investing in the future. Start with using the scorecard to identify and initiate small transformations in your operations, then use it to guide future decisions and strategies to keep your firm moving in the direction of ever-increasing sustainability—and toward unexpectedly innovative and valuable solutions.

Chapter 1

Lies about Sustainability Courtesy of the Status Quo

The stone age didn't end for lack of stones.

—*Sheikh Zaki Yamani*

In the late third century, the great Greek king Pyrrhus of Epirus, Italy (then part of Greece), defended a small town in southern Italy from an impending invasion by the Romans. Tarantum was small, but mighty, founded by the Spartans. During the period of Greek colonization, it flourished, becoming a cultural, economic, and military power. It was the birthplace of several important philosophers, statesmen, writers, and athletes of the time.

Meanwhile, Pyrrhus was known to be one of the most skilled generals of the time. Pyrrhus defended Tarantum well; however, the victory was accompanied by large military losses. It resulted in not only a significant depletion of Pyrrhus's troops but also the loss of many of his skilled leaders. According to Greek philosopher and biographer Plutarch, Pyrrhus remarked, "If we are victorious in one more battle with the Romans, we shall be utterly ruined." And so it came to pass.[1]

Tarantum rose victorious; however, the forge was so significantly depleted thereafter that the city was unable to withstand further assault from the Romans, and it fell a few years later. Since then, the expression *a Pyrrhic victory* has come to mean an accomplishment accompanied by such heavy losses that the value of the win is negated by the outcome of the victory itself. In other words, one has waged a duel against oneself.[2] Sound familiar?

It's easy enough to make the argument that the "advances" we have achieved in the last two hundred years represent a Pyrrhic victory for humankind. Our current-day economic activities are in direct conflict with human health and environmental viability. But is it true that technological and economic progress necessitates the destruction of our natural world? Or is that just one of the lies the status quo tells us to preserve itself?

The research certainly proves the status quo wrong.

According to the Yale Climate Connections Initiative, a 4.5-degree rise in global surface temperature (as opposed to a 2.1-degree rise that will be attained if the world meets net zero goals) will cost us $224 billion per year—three-quarters of which will be related to health impacts.[3] More than a third of that $224 billion is attributed to an increase in heat-related deaths.[4] Furthermore, an MIT study on infrastructural impacts of climate change found that "infrastructure expenditures may rise as much as 25 percent due to climate change alone" by 2090.[5] What this tells us is that environmental considerations are truly not a barrier to economic progress—but ignoring them is.

Economists of the future will surely consider our focus on short-term gains at the expense of environmental and social factors and a lack of will to develop new and innovative sustainable solutions as a Pyrrhic victory. In the absence of bold solutions to create economic value along the triple bottom line (financial, environmental, and social), the losses incurred by organizations due to climate-related shocks will be so monumental that they will negate any value obtained from the victory itself.

There is a way of achieving the same high returns and scalability of our ventures without destroying our planet—the source of the resources on which our economic activities rely. We can achieve superior performance, convenience, efficiency, and profitability not in spite of a focus on sustainability but because of it. And if superior performance and profitability in sustainable products are possible, then perhaps the power to achieve global climate-change goals is also within our reach.

We fully believe that business leaders do not have to accept toxic consequences to our loved ones' health as a by-product of their economic activities. In this chapter, we audit a mosaic of so-called successful firms, industry actions, and products, and suggest more sustainable alternatives in order to prove that green-based solutions can deliver higher performance than their traditional counterparts *and* perform better on financial metrics over the long term.

Let's start with the environment's number one offender: plastics.

Lie 1: We Use Cheap Toxic Materials over Expensive Harmless Ones

No industry sector or product is as polarizing as plastics. According to the Plastics Industry Association, US plastics accounted for an estimated $432 billion in shipments and over nine hundred thousand jobs in 2017.[6] In 1996, plastics accounted for approximately $275 billion in shipments, which at the time was a 55 percent increase since 1991.[7] The most valuable features of plastics are their versatility and durability. Furthermore, the relative inertness of plastics lends to their being ideal candidates for everything from packaging and containers to drug delivery mechanisms. From a healthcare perspective, it is literally a life-saving material. Yet the long-term accumulation of plastic polymers in our groundwater and environment is toxic. And the energy-intensive manufacturing process does the earth no favors either.

The plastics manufacturing process requires prolonged heating and cooling phases: heating to create the polymerization, and cooling to maximize the yield. If only the manufacturing process could occur at room temperature and pressure, it would minimize both the use of a significant amount of fossil fuel and the resulting pollution. Another green hurdle is that batch plastics are often created "off-specification." This results in large volumes of one-use products—and a lot of waste.

What is it really that's stopping us from introducing "greener" pathways for plastic production without compromising profitability?

After all, catalysts already exist that can reduce the pollution associated with plastic production by speeding up chemical reactions and lowering energy demands. Using them would make the industry not only more environmentally sustainable but also more cost-efficient. Further, real-time monitoring technology is currently available to prevent the production of potentially unviable plastics—less waste meets sustainability and profitability goals! And to reduce the toxicity of plastics on degradation, scientists have already developed a method to produce plastics from sugar and carbon dioxide rather than the carcinogenic benzene and toluene feedstocks that are currently used. Unlike their non-biodegradable counterparts, sugar- and carbon-based plastics break down to their component parts when exposed to the enzymes present in soil and can be combined without the high heat and pressure of traditional plastics.

Less-toxic products: check.

Lower-cost production: check.

If the solutions to some of these issues exist, why haven't they been implemented yet? There are a few reasons for this:

- Lack of awareness of what is possible. It is probable that you've never heard of green chemistry. Are we correct? While green chemistry solutions have created profitability and significant success stories for most of the world's leading organizations, the lack of mainstream information on the subject is a likely barrier to systematic implementation. After all, you can't implement what you don't know exists . . .

- Capital investment strategies typically align with solutions that are based on application-driven digital platforms. While this is certainly an important trend for several reasons, most of the world's production processes are dependent on material and energy loops. This lack of focus on infrastructure, hardware, and other material and energy-loop considerations has likely limited the mainstreaming of green chemistry and green engineering solutions.

- Allocation of research and development. Traditionally, we find that investment dollars are concentrated in a few sectors globally, such as healthcare and the life sciences. By contrast, infrastructure, commodities, and manufacturing in general typically lack sophisticated research and development funding and capabilities.

But what if the plastics breakthrough was just a fluke? Surely there must be more than one industry in which sustainable products and processes are cheaper, demonstrate more profitable margins, and are also better for the environment. There is: cement.

Lie 2: Green Products Cost More for a Poorer Experience

A hallmark of civilization is the durability and flawlessness of its buildings, roads, and walkways. For millennia, cement has literally been the foundation of civilization. In the past century, Portland cement has become the global standard in cement use. If you've ever driven on a highway, strolled on a sidewalk, or entered a tall building, you have been on Portland cement. Unfortunately, Portland cement is extremely harmful for the environment.

The cement industry, along with the oil and gas industry, has been identified as a "carbon major" industry, with seven entities producing

13.21 percent of the world's global annual carbon dioxide–equivalent emissions between 1854 and 2010.[8] Cement production alone contributes 8 percent to the total carbon dioxide emissions in the world.[9] Yet the material is here to stay. Researchers say it's the key ingredient for satisfying global housing and modern infrastructure needs.[10] In a McKinsey and Company analysis of the cement industry's impact on the global carbon footprint, the analysts found that "the cement industry alone is responsible for about a quarter of all industry CO_2 emissions, and it also generates the most CO_2 emissions per dollar of revenue."[11]

Perhaps you are starting to see the pattern here, one that we hope to reverse with the Sustainability Scorecard. The world's commitment to the status quo has allowed far too many unsustainable processes to remain undisrupted for literally centuries—for example, Portland cement; the Haber-Bosch process for the production of ammonia-based fertilizer, which we will discuss later; and the internal combustion engine used by Henry Ford that continues to demonstrate low fuel efficiency. Why? It certainly isn't because of the unavailability of other, more sustainable options. Such as Ferrock™.

What if instead of emitting carbon dioxide, cement could absorb it? Ferrock, developed and patented by Dr. David Stone in 2014, does exactly this.

As a PhD student at the University of Arizona, Stone was working on an experiment to prevent iron from rusting when he serendipitously stumbled on the discovery of a material that seemed to bubble and froth. He thought the project was a waste, but when he returned the next day, he found that the material had turned into hard stone. He had developed a carbon-negative material that could substitute for Portland cement.

Ferrock presents several advantages over its predecessor. Steel dust (a nonrecyclable by-product of steel production) and silica, which can be collected from landfills, are part of the entirely "green" chemical process used in its production. The cement also has higher compressive strength than Portland cement, better crack resistance, higher tolerance to extreme heat (an important feature in a hotter world), and lower production costs at high scale. The secret of this material may be its proportions of calcium and silicate, which "enhance the strength of the material, reduce material volume and cut the emissions associated with concrete by more than half."[12]

To test these claims, four graduate students at the University of Southern California conducted a life-cycle analysis of Ferrock. They concluded that the manufacturing process is much less energy intensive than for Portland cement because it does not require any heat to catalyze the curing process.[13] (Conversely, the manufacturing process of Portland cement requires subjecting limestone to 2,800 degrees Fahrenheit.) The end result is a net-negative carbon output and a cement-like product that increases in hardness as it absorbs carbon.

Another material study compared the environmental impacts of ordinary Portland cement and Ferrock focusing especially on factors such as the products' water use, energy consumption, and contribution to carbon pollution.[14] By substituting ordinary Portland cement with Ferrock in varying proportions in concrete, scientists are trying to find the optimum ratio of replacement that yields desired results in terms of both strength (compressive, split tensile, and flexural tested) and sustainability. In all the test results, the addition of Ferrock not only produced a significant increase in strength but also outperformed on sustainability factors.

To test widespread integration of this product as a cement replacement, IronKast, David Stone's firm, has received grants from the Environmental Protection Agency (EPA) to assist with the Tohono O'odham Community College's (TOCC) Tribal Eco Ambassador Program.[15] The Tohono O'odham nation is a Native American tribe in the Sonora desert in Arizona. The TOCC's Tribal Eco Ambassador Program is a partnership between the EPA and the American Indian Higher Education Consortium, linking tribal college university professors and students with EPA scientists to solve the environmental problems most important to their communities.[16] It has led to the construction of Ferrock building blocks manufactured from local recycled glass and steel for sidewalks and ramps. In fact, the community college's patio was entirely constructed with Ferrock, utilizing fifty thousand glass bottles and several tons of steel dust that would have been dumped in the community landfill.

But Ferrock is not the only "green" cement that performs better and costs less to produce. Another firm, Solidia, has made early strides with carbon-negative cement by replacing a key ingredient, limestone, with another synthetic. Not only is it cheaper and faster to produce than traditional cement, it is also carbon negative, producing 70 percent less in emissions during its life cycle.[17] Interestingly for the cement industry, which is facing increasing pressure from investors and governments to decarbonize, the biggest hurdle to mainstream adoption of these sustainable cements is the threat to traditional cement plants.[18] Decommissioning them would eventually render them as distressed assets on financial statements. Distressed assets, in particular, are an outcome that operations and financial professionals are eager to avoid due to the implication that the capital invested in the produced goods cannot be recovered, and will be recorded as a loss on financial statements. Here the challenge of overcoming shut-down economics is the primary barrier to scaling. Innovation that is more efficient and higher performing than existing solutions threatens to shut down the economics of an entire industry. In this case, what is likely to be more practical in terms of a business application are drop-in solutions that can reduce the overall carbon-intensive nature of cement rather than a solution that would outright render existing practices obsolete.

The Status Quo Preserves Itself

Consider some of the twenty-first-century absurdities we live with today—things that individuals fifty to one hundred years from now will look back on and remark with correct judgment as our absurdities and obscenities: toxic preservatives in baby food, fertilizers, and cleaning products; air pollution from unfiltered vehicle emissions; and microplastics, to name a few. These things are so blatantly flawed in thought that it taxes our imagination to see why they are considered acceptable in today's climate.

Now think about the processes that produce some of the most common products today. Some of the most embedded and seemingly innocuous products are created from toxic processes that have remained undisrupted for decades, and in many cases centuries. Like plastics. Like cement.

Why do we put up with them?

Our status quo bias, our irrational preference for the current state of affairs, our shortsightedness, is affecting our decision-making. It is fostering intellectual inertia, placing a higher value on embedded capital than on short- and long-term investments that could open new markets, capture previously untapped market segments, or even innovate-out competitors.

Every time a new technology, process, or innovation is rejected because it would disrupt the mechanism by which current processes run, that is the status quo preserving itself.

Every time firms forgo the opportunity to integrate innovative ideas that are better for the financial, social, and environmental bottom line in order to preserve the capital in existing supply chains, that is the existing supply chain preserving itself.

The message that we are hearing loud and clear from the status quo is that the only way to replicate the economic growth of yesterday is to keep doing what we've always done: employ an operating model wherein resources are considered infinite and passively accept the negative consequences that we are scaling.

And it simply isn't so. We've been duped into believing that success requires harm (in the form of negative environmental or human health externalities) because we are living in a future designed by those before us, who assumed that trade-offs between social, environmental, and financial factors must occur for economic activities to be profitable. They did not consider that exponential growth in economic activity, coupled with an aging and increasing human population, would result in climate-change-related economic shocks. Take economist Milton Friedman.

In his 1962 book *Capitalism and Freedom*, Friedman expressed the idea that the social responsibility of business is to increase its profits.[19] This idea was further socialized by way of his *New York Times Magazine* article in 1970 in which he wrote that firms that concern themselves with community rather than profit lend themselves to totalitarianism. Lies.

If all we are doing is maximizing shareholder wealth, we will take the shortest route to the end result, even if that end result comprises several negative consequences such as pollution, toxicity, and climate change—but hey, why fix it if it ain't broke? Well, it's broken.

At this stage of our economic life cycle, it is clear that addressing environmental and societal issues are key to businesses' long-term existence, and significant management research and industry success stories exist regarding the curvilinear relationship between environmental and social governance (henceforth referred to as ESG) and financial profitability. ESG is a common term used by investors to indicate a firm's performance on environmental, social, and governance related factors. Of course, management of the material and energy inputs that create the products and services firms sell to increase their profits is critical to their future operations and financial health. If material and energy resources were to run out, the interconnected supply chains that power our economy would also cease to exist.

Christine Bader, author of *The Evolution of a Corporate Idealist: When Girl Meets Oil* and Amazon's director of social responsibility from 2015 to 2017, has a much more comprehensive and truthful view of capitalism than Friedman's. She envisions a model in which businesses adopt metrics and principles that embed the environment and human rights into how they do business, in which "pro-social behavior is good for companies and society alike."[20]

Let's broaden our view to look at all aspects of the financial benefits—not just profits and expenses but also market share, sources of origination of revenue streams, a full perspective of cost accounting, and so on. As this chapter shows, inherently sustainable products and processes can lead to additional revenue streams, capture new markets or consumers, and decrease customer acquisition costs. These income-related benefits are further bolstered by expense reductions related to waste management and the handling of toxic materials. But these various benefits are realized only when firms and leaders challenge their status quos and invest intellectually in redesigning current systems to integrate meaningful innovation.

Social Responsibility *Is* Fiduciary Responsibility

It is intellectually more complex and operationally more challenging to design and implement inherently sustainable solutions in established organizations. This is inherently the case because creating circular systems and ensuring that all outputs ultimately either degrade safely or serve as inputs is a process design challenge. So challenging, in fact, that most of our current day processes are linear in nature. However, if you consider the cost of toxic waste management, transport, storage, and disposal and of potential litigation due to worker safety issues, building resilience into existing operations is a cost-saving measure that is well worth our time. Socially and environmentally responsible practices must be perceived as an investment, just as any other investment, to truly compute return on investment when embedded into the products and services core to corporate activity. For example, when supply chain transparency is embedded into the process, forced labor practices and environmentally extractive strategies are innovated out. This ultimately helps us arrive at the true cost of goods sold (rather, the true cost of doing business). In addition, the return on investment along environmental lines could result in regenerative inputs that ultimately decrease the total cost of production and even higher market share due to increased customer uptake (because of aligned business and customer values). Business continuity and the maximizing of shareholder wealth necessitate that material and energy flows remain intact for future economic activity. In other words, social responsibility *is* fiduciary responsibility and an act that ensures maximizing of shareholder wealth. We cannot survive without it.

In so many other aspects of business, companies that resist transformation become dinosaurs. The same goes for sustainability. Consumers are demanding more environmentally benign and nontoxic products, and leaders can no longer remain blind to the risk of disruption by competitors that can truly do better things—rather than just doing things better.

In the next chapters, we'll show you how to create successful transformations that will embed sustainability into your corporate strategy and align your firm with the consumer of tomorrow while deftly managing the short-term consequences. That's where the Sustainability Scorecard and its principles for managing and scaling sustainability come in. This science-backed path forward is the way you make it less organizationally and operationally complicated to move continuously in the direction of increasing sustainability.

Chapter 2

The Four Principles for Managing and Scaling Sustainability

> Problems cannot be solved at the same level that created them.
>
> —*Albert Einstein*

With pressure on firms to innovate and disrupt themselves, there has been a rush into the sustainability space in all industries. Great news, right? Actually, the reality is more like a lot of businesses doing the right thing—providing products that are better for human health and the environment—wrong.

Here's one example. Retail firms are leveraging their strong consumer relationships and multiple locations to serve as drop-off sites for clothing recycling. Sounds like a win-win-win for consumers, clothing manufacturers, and the earth; however, these retail giants are ill-suited for handling the volume of unwanted textiles they receive.

The recycling process weakens the clothing fibers, resulting in a lower-quality output that either forms part of the (unsustainable) fast fashion production model or, worse, is totally unusable. In fact, it is common for less than 0.7 percent of the recycled clothes to be used in the creation of a new outfit.[1] With all this energy being expended to arrive at a product not fit for retail, it makes you wonder whether sending your old clothes straight to the landfill might be the more earth-friendly option.

Consider also the use of biofuels derived from agricultural crops, an example that Julie Zimmerman, professor of green engineering at Yale School of the Environment, shared with students of her PhD alma mater, the University of Michigan, in 2014. Zimmerman is an internationally recognized engineer whose work is focused on advancing innovations in sustainable technologies. She and Paul collaboratively established the fundamental framework for her field with her seminal publications on the Twelve Principles of Green Engineering in 2003.

In her talk at the University of Michigan, she told the story of the rise and fall of corn-based ethanol. Once upon a time, corn-based ethanol was viewed as the bright, shining hope in the dark, dismal landscape of fighting climate change. It's a renewable fuel with feedstock requiring only six months to grow. The growing of corn creates jobs in the agriculture sector. And the biofuel can be concentrated up to 10 percent, giving it great generalizability among most vehicles. For others, a few alterations to the engine allowed for easy compatibility.[2]

In hindsight, we learned that the widespread production of corn causes water-quality issues arising from fertilizer application, a decrease in food exports and a consequent increase in food prices, and deforestation leading to additional climate impacts. Even though the end product may have been competitive with traditional gasoline, from a supply-chain and system design perspective, corn-based ethanol was not a sustainable solution at all.[3]

One last example: photovoltaic cells, otherwise known as solar cells or PVs. If nature is solar powered and if we can design cells to store and transmit solar energy to homes, isn't that a move in the right direction? You'd think so, but no. Generating electricity with solar panels can in fact be more harmful to the environment than good. The process actually releases more greenhouse gases than burning coal.[4]

The business case for PVs was initially a tough sell. In the 1950s, the cells had an efficiency of approximately 4 percent. Incremental increases in efficiency and declining prices with scale led to widespread adoption in geographies suited for solar. This, alongside a reputation for leading the clean-energy movement, has contributed to the perception that scaling PVs is not only a lucrative market but also aligned with the social and environmental values of its consumers. In reality, there are multiple areas where PVs fall short of perceived benefits.[5]

As it turns out, the manufacture of these cells results in large-scale leaching and chemical pollution leading to public health hazards. There is also a great deal of variability in performance of the cells depending on the technology used. Thin-film PVs and utility-scale PVs are known to be low on efficiency, which is compensated for during installation with greater land use—which leads to land loss. Its life-cycle analysis also shows that the energy to mine the raw materials used in these cells (e.g., quartz, sand for silicon, and zinc and copper for metal-grade cadmium and tellurium, respectively) can be quite high. It can take 20 to 30 percent longer to "pay back" the energy used to manufacture PV cells than for traditional fuel cells. This, by the way, is why firms prefer to manufacture rather than recover their "lost" e-waste from landfills—because their inflow of rare-earth metals is faster than their inroads in the supply-chain market for recovery of e-waste from landfills.[6]

What these examples show is that doing the right thing wrong is an easy mistake to make—and it doesn't serve our purposes at all. So how can we ensure that the sustainability solutions we are working to design, implement, and scale are themselves inherently sustainable? How can we know we are doing the right things right . . . or at the very least, doing better things better?

Doing the Right Things Right

The first step in designing a sustainable operating model is to learn how to recognize when the right thing is being done wrong. Recognition is critical. But with the rise of several different certifications and attestations to the level of sustainability of various products, it can be confusing and even impractical to assess the long supply chains associated with every product line at a large organization. At some point, supply chains become opaque, and it can be difficult to trace the origin of component inputs of the supply chain from different parts of the world, with sourcing passing through various suppliers, vendors, subcontractors, and assemblers. In addition, the ideal audit of an entire supply chain includes an assessment of labor practices. This can be done to a degree with vendors who disclose their practices and meet certain certifications, but what happens when your supplies come from regions of the world where disclosure is not mandated or performed?

Tim Mohin is the former CEO of Global Reporting Institute, which set the first global standards for sustainability reporting, and the author of the books *Changing Business from the Inside Out* and *A Tree-Hugger's Guide to Working in Corporations*. He famously slept in dormitories and spent his days in factories to obtain a firsthand account of Apple's supply chain and labor conditions in its Chinese operations. But not all firms can afford to send corporate social responsibility (CSR) executives across the world for surprise labor practice and materials audits. So what do you do when your organization is constrained by such boundaries? Where does the tracing stop for each component? How can we realistically develop "farm-to-table" supply chains for businesses without jumping down a global rabbit hole each time? There are several solutions that we will get into; however, technological solutions such as those offered by the Queen of Raw, Stephanie Benedetto, to create supply-chain transparency in the fashion industry go a long way in enabling visibility and securing trust by way of a blockchain solution.

The question of system boundaries and constraints is inherent to sustainability, and always top of mind for sustainability management students as they plan life-cycle scenarios. These challenges are big—but so are the consequences of allowing unsustainable practices to persist in your supply chains. And that is why the need for the Sustainability Scorecard and its principles has never been greater. Next, we'll explain the origin of these science-backed principles.

The Twelve Principles of Green Chemistry

We based the sustainability management principles on the Twelve Principles of Green Chemistry that Paul and his partner at the EPA, Dr. John Warner, developed in 1998. Green chemistry is the utilization of a set of principles that reduces or entirely eliminates the use and/or generation of harmful substances in the design, manufacture, and application of chemical products. The call to action in this branch of chemistry is to develop entirely new and unexpected chemical reactions that create products and processes that are environmentally benign and safe for human health, in addition to creating resource efficiency, energy efficiency, and operational safety. Green chemistry is applied robustly in industry and in research and development today. High schools hold Olympiads to test the knowledge and skills of students, and various awards recognize the impact of this field in industrial ecology and economics. The Green Chemistry Challenge, also known as the Presidential Green Chemistry Awards, was started by the EPA in 1996 to "promote the environmental and economic benefit of developing novel green chemistry."

The Twelve Principles of Green Chemistry bring design thinking and complex problem-solving strategies up front in the "discovery" phase of product and process design. They have led to the design of countless processes that not only achieve superior performance goals but do so in a manner that is environmentally benign and nontoxic. (Accepting anything less is, as Paul likes to say, absurd.)

THE TWELVE PRINCIPLES OF GREEN CHEMISTRY

1. Waste prevention
2. Atom economization
3. Reduced hazardous chemical synthesis
4. Design of safer chemicals
5. Safer solvents and auxiliaries usage
6. Design for energy efficiency
7. Use of renewable feedstocks
8. Reduction of derivatives
9. Catalysis
10. Design for degradation
11. Real-time analysis for pollution prevention
12. Creation of inherently safer chemistry for accident prevention

The principles serve as a "how to" for chemists globally in the innovative design of unexpected solutions. They have been adopted by the EPA in the US, global multilaterals such as the United Nations and World Health Organization with a focus on sustainable development goals, and educational institutions. Through the years of the Green Chemistry Challenge, disruptive firms have used the principles to achieve unexpected, seemingly impossible goals, including the following:

- The elimination of 830 million pounds of hazardous chemicals and solvents each year—enough to fill almost 3,800 railroad tank cars or a train nearly 47 miles long.
- Saving 21 billion gallons of water each year—an amount roughly equivalent to the amount used by 980,000 people annually.
- The elimination of 7.8 billion pounds of carbon dioxide equivalents from being released into the air each year—equal to taking 770,000 automobiles off the road.[7]

While leading visionary firms can demonstrate countless excellent examples of commercialization, those innovations have not been systematically incorporated, and they have not been translated into business management principles until now.

The economy of the future will have fundamentally different levers than those that got us to this point today. The future will require a triple-bottom-line approach—that is, an approach that is circular and requires ESG-related value propositions. We drew on the Twelve Principles of Green Chemistry to provide management leaders of tomorrow a scientifically derived framework by which to implement and profit from sustainability.

The Four Principles for Managing and Scaling Sustainability

Chemistry is an exact science. As Paul often states, "Chemicals are dumb; they know not what they do." To that end, following the Twelve Principles of Green Chemistry enables scientists, researchers, and developers to create new, unexpected solutions by creatively manipulating these chemicals.

However, these disruptive new technologies need to be successfully implemented into organizations. Smaller, more agile start-ups may be able to more easily scale such innovative solutions, but first they need to prove the viability of those solutions in order to raise adequate funding. Meanwhile, large organizations with embedded capital (financial and human) will need a more deliberate approach to adopting new solutions in order to manage the short-term effects on operations and their balance sheets. The Four Principles for Managing and Scaling Sustainability and the Sustainability Scorecard offer a proven path forward for both types of firms.

Jeff Sonnenfeld, management guru and founder of the Chief Executive Leadership Institute at Yale University, states that one of the strongest indicators of an environmental focus in corporate strategy is the creation of an executive-level sustainability position: chief sustainability officer (CSO).[8] The CSO is responsible for applying scientific advances to industry in "the right way"—the way that leads to an increasingly sustainable *and* profitable future. We developed these principles for CSOs, operations-focused leaders, strategy and innovation professionals, and anyone else looking to make sustainability a strategic priority, complete with metrics to measure the principles' business success. We did so by consulting and collaborating with hundreds of industry leaders working to innovate processes and products in a manner that was financially and operationally forward looking. And now, here they are. (We'll discuss the Sustainability Scorecard—the metrics by which to measure your sustainability progress—in the next chapter.)

> Principle 1: Waste prevention
> Principle 2: Maximizing efficiency and performance
> Principle 3: Using renewable inputs
> Principle 4: Ensuring safe degradation

Any product or process that fulfills all the principles will be inherently sustainable and profitable. New products and processes that follow the principles will also be inherently "unexpected," as these constraints have never been embedded into the design process before. Next we dive into each of the principles to explain how.

Principle 1: Waste Prevention

GOALS

- Prevent waste from entering terminating graveyards
- Eliminate hazards
- Close material loops to maximally recover the economic value of the material inputs

Many of today's manufacturing processes follow a linear path wherein inputs are pushed through a production chain that results in the creation of products and by-products that are either unintentionally persistent or toxic. In fact, many processes produce waste at a much higher quantity or concentration than the actual product they are designed to create. But what if manufacturers sought sustainable growth by creating closed-loop systems, with the by-products being neither toxic nor waste but having their own value? Later in the book we'll discuss a very cool company that is doing just that with its carbon dioxide waste.

You may have noticed that we have used the term *e-factor* previously in this book. E-factor is simply the weight of waste produced in relation to the weight of the desired product. Therefore, empirically, the principle states that the concept of waste must entirely disappear from the process design frameworks and supply chains of the future. Whether in terms of material flow or energy, the goal is to generate value from each by-product of the process. True sustainability requires firms to address waste generation at every stage of a product's life cycle, including what happens at the end of its life. (Upcycling may extend a product's useful life, but if it still eventually ends up in a landfill, there's more progress to be made.)

When thinking about waste prevention, one of the first areas to study is waste generation—for example, by tracking the weight of the raw materials that will be disposed of at the end of the production cycle. In various industries, this can take the shape of tracking the amount of "active" ingredient that made its way into the final product in proportion to the weights of all the inputs. A focus on waste generation lends itself to exploring various process improvements—for example, process efficiency, speed of reaction (in the case of chemical manufacturing), and the use of alternative raw material inputs that increase yield without compromising performance. The other major consideration is end-of-life management: What happens to the product when it is no longer useful? Where does it end up—recycling, landfill, compost—and what's the impact? End-of-life management requires that you understand the categories and weights of the materials that can be recovered and re-entered into production as inputs or even upcycled into new products.

Principle 2: Maximizing Efficiency and Performance

GOALS

- Create products/materials and process energy and material inputs efficiently
- Expand the definition of *high performance* to include "benign by design" and being nontoxic to human health and the environment (i.e., nondepleting, nontoxic, and nonpersistent)

In the past, performance was viewed almost entirely as the ability to efficiently accomplish a narrowly defined function (e.g., the number of pests killed per certain volume of pesticide). But, as we know, this focus solely on function or on achievement of a single goal has led to the creation of numerous pesticides that not only eliminate pests but pose significant health hazards to humans and the environment. Perhaps the focus is on an anesthetic gas, a dye of a certain shade, or the ability of a vehicle to accelerate to high speeds in minimal time. Performance has to date focused singularly on desirable qualities and thereby driven a singular focus to achieve them.

What should performance mean today? And what constitutes an operations process that yields high-performing products?

With this principle, we are broadening the definition of performance to include all of the aspects that we care about in addition to function—particularly the elimination of negative externalities related to human and environmental health. For process designers, this means understanding the functional specs of the end product and also the hazardous downstream effects of the process, the waste generated, and the product itself to make sure they are nondepleting, nontoxic, and nonpersistent in the environment.

Consider a chemical plant. Traditionally, measuring the performance of a chemical plant would take into account the efficiency of production and viable storage of the end product. With respect to production, this can typically include metrics such as machine downtime, batch production cycle times, or error mitigation (loss of a produced batch of chemicals if it is out of specification). An expansion of the definition of performance for this scenario would include the efficient removal of externalities related to chemical safety for the environment and worker health.

Traditional solutions to increase site safety include pipe enhancements, security-related enhancements such as interlocks and access control, and even accessibility to respirators for worker safety. However, if a new, more sustainable solution in this scenario is considered, how does that change the product? If a system is to not only deliver high performance but also ensure safety and financial feasibility, the answer could lie in inherent site safety. That is, a chemical plant with an inherently safe structure would not need to rely on regular assessments, maintenance upgrades to pipes, and the like, and would thus prevent ongoing year-over-year operating costs and procurement of replacement equipment.

In 2016, an erroneous chemical reaction at a manufacturing and storage facility in Atchison, Kansas, resulted in the production of a toxic cloud that exposed more than 140 individuals to toxic chlorine gas that can damage lung tissue, and led to a shelter-in-place warning for thousands of others in the community. According to a study by the National Association of Chemical Distributors, more than thirty-nine million metric tons of the product were delivered to the community every 8.4 seconds.[9] To improve the performance of this facility, the firm introduced safer and greener processes that led to the elimination of several toxic bulk chemicals and the phasing out of another chemical. These eliminations and the design of a safer, greener process led to inherent safety of the site, making the plant's functionality safe in and of itself, and resulted in significant operating cost savings for the firm.

The introduction of inherent safety as a design mechanism or product specification expands the definition of performance to reach beyond function and encapsulate environmental and human health externalities, and reduces worker safety expenses and overall operating expenses related to handling, storing, and transport of chemicals. Traditional mechanisms for ensuring site safety (such as pipe enhancements to prevent leaks) are certainly effective safety measures, but they appear to be less optimal solutions (financially and in terms of performance) than the "unexpected solution" of inherently safe chemical plants that leverage green chemicals. These plants would be safe even in the event of a leak and therefore are not only safer but also more cost effective.

Principle 3: Using Renewable Inputs

GOALS

- Create circularity in the energy system
- Minimize or negate the use of depleting resources for energy

One of the key messages we want you to take away from this book is that material and energy inputs are a major influence on the sustainability of products, processes, and systems. Inherently sustainable systems cannot be created without a strong focus on material inputs and how they impact sustainability at each stage of a product's life cycle. For example, biological inputs, though renewable, also produce waste as a by-product. What about leveraging that waste to serve as an input and to create circularity in the energy system (i.e., to close the energy loop)?

Supplier diversity can help in making sure a firm has access to renewable inputs without any disruption in business continuity (because if one person can't provide something, another person will). Streamlining inventory and managing complexity are other complementary tactics. In particular, the diversity of mineral inputs can be minimized for ease of recoverability, value retention, and disassembly.

Principle 4: Ensuring Safe Degradation

GOALS

- Safely disintegrate components using nontoxic products and processes
- Ensure that disintegrated components are nontoxic to humans and the environment

Vast numbers of synthetic chemicals are used in everyday consumer products that routinely expose large populations to toxic chemicals for long periods of time—especially if the product is used on a daily basis. For example, phthalates are widely used to increase the flexibility of plastics, but also disrupt human hormonal balance. And organophosphates are highly effective insect repellents, but are severely neurotoxic to mammals.

Unintended biological or environmental effects can be avoided through the use of safe substitutions that are functionally equivalent but less of a concern from a safety standpoint. That's where safe degradation comes in. Abidance with this principle ensures that hazardous chemicals do not persist in the environment. (Persistence leads to bioaccumulation—the accumulation of toxic chemicals into human and animal bodies either through air, water, or food intake, or directly through the skin.)

Toxicology knowledge is essential to identifying chemicals that degrade safely and designing out molecular features that are the basis for hazards. Fortunately, there are databases and models that evaluate biodegradability and can be used to evaluate the sustainability and toxicity of chemical inputs.

Another important consideration for fulfilling this principle is the safe separation of components. For example, many conventional methods for recovering materials from products at the end of their lives require the use of hazardous solvents or the use of high heat and energy. Addressing safe end-of-life recovery up front in the design phase for safe end-of-life recovery can also yield significant financial benefits for firms by way of decreased waste and waste management efforts and reduced processing time for recovery.

Onward and Upward

The Four Principles for Managing and Scaling Sustainability can be applied to firms at any stage of their sustainability journey, whether they are established, market-leading firms; new start-ups; or any size in between. In the next chapter, we will dive deep into the Sustainability Scorecard, which uses metrics based on the sustainability management principles to assist firms in

- Designing and refining their sustainability strategy
- Prioritizing future initiatives
- Developing additional firm-specific sustainability metrics that are truly forward facing

Let's go!

Chapter 3

The Sustainability Scorecard

The difference between what we do and what we are capable of doing would suffice to solve most of the world's problems

—*Mahatma Gandhi*

I n Paul's MBA class, a student once asked about sustainability management, "So ultimately, are we just talking about risk management?"

The short and yet complete answer is no.

It is clear that CEOs are thinking about the role of their firms in society and as stewards of the environment from which they draw their inputs. They are saying it is no longer enough to be "just good enough" by meeting minimum compliance requirements or achieving high-quality metrics. The call to action globally is to create "products that are better for you and better for the environment." But this high standard cannot be achieved through error containment or risk avoidance alone.

In sustainability-focused discussions at round-table meetings with executives, we often hear them express their understanding that climate is connected to water, water to land, land to air, and so forth, and that their risk-based methodologies just cannot seem to keep up with the various fatalities and failures that are likely at every one of those nexuses. Yet they'll invariably say, after acknowledging their understanding of the interconnected nature of their supply chains' shock patterns, "Well, so I think I'll just have to focus on reducing my carbon footprint."

The lack of a systemic approach to measuring, tracking, and reporting sustainability KPIs drives outcome-focused leaders either to focus on the one metric they likely can control (a lot of times, that's carbon) or to just go back to playing whack-a-mole with risk-based avoidance behavior. So for a firm with a heavy utilization of water, for example, water stewardship and conservation become high-priority risk-related items in its sustainability strategy. For agricultural firms, land use and soil quality become high-priority risk-related items in their models.

To be clear, risk management is important, and ESG audits will go a long way in ensuring compliance and a focus on the holistic impact of business operations (versus just impact on the financial bottom line), but sustainability strategies embedded in risk management propagate an avoidance behavior. This works right up to when it doesn't—right up to when the volume of low-probability high-cost events or high-probability high-cost events is too high to address, and the risks outlined in the SEC filings outline numerous interconnected issues that reduce investor confidence.

Of course, established risk management metrics are important to track, especially in the initial phase of a firm's sustainability journey. But in order to scale from a pilot or small venture to a midsize firm, and then from a midsize to a large or even global enterprise, forward-looking strategic approaches and metrics are what's necessary. *Strategic* is the operative word here, because in order to look forward and design for the future, a firm cannot live in the past. We recommend driving forward with new metrics that are rooted not in avoidance behavior but in managing and scaling sustainability—hence the Sustainability Score-card. And for your business to do this work over the long run, we rec-ommend using a compass rather than a speedometer. In other words, it's about your direction, not your speed. This is how you make sus-tainability work for your business—with incremental transformations that account for the financial and operational trade-offs while continu-ing to move your business in the direction of greater sustainability.

The Sustainability Scorecard Key Performance Indicators

SCORECARD COMPONENT: WASTE PREVENTION

KPI	SUB-METRIC	PRODUCT/ PROCESS 1 BEFORE SUSTAINABILITY TRANSFORMATION	PRODUCT/ PROCESS 2 UNEXPECTED SOLUTION: SUSTAINABLE EARTH	RATING
Economy of waste	Atom economy (in g/mol, percentage)			
	E-factor			
	Packaging: percentage of readily recyclable material			
Economy of space	Number of units per square foot of product			

SCORECARD COMPONENT: WASTE PREVENTION
(continued)

KPI	SUB-METRIC	PRODUCT/PROCESS 1 BEFORE SUSTAINABILITY TRANSFORMATION	PRODUCT/PROCESS 2 UNEXPECTED SOLUTION: SUSTAINABLE EARTH	RATING
	Number of units transported per vehicle			
Process intensification	Productivity/size ratio Productivity/weight ratio			

- 0: process recovers *all* (91%–100% by weight) the waste generated.
- 1: process has a *majority* (51%–90% by weight) of its waste recovered through upcycling, landfill-based recovery processes/safe degradation in a graveyard, and/or multiple-use mechanisms ultimately avoiding a graveyard at end of life.
- 2: process has a *majority* of its waste disposed through the landfill, autoclaving, or incineration.
- 3: process leverages graveyards as its sole end of life (91%–100%).

SCORECARD COMPONENT: MAXIMIZING EFFICIENCY AND PERFORMANCE

KPI	SUB-METRIC	PRODUCT/ PROCESS 1 BEFORE SUSTAINABILITY TRANSFORMATION	PRODUCT/ PROCESS 2 UNEXPECTED SOLUTION: SUSTAINABLE EARTH	R A T I N G
Material efficiency	Mass of recycled material/total mass			
	Mass of renewable material/total mass			
Environmental health metrics	Global warming potential (in kg CO_2 emissions)			
	Acidification potential (in kg CO_2 emissions)			
	Eutrophica-tion potential (in kg N emissions)			
	Ozone depletion potential (in kg CDC 11 emissions)			

SCORECARD COMPONENT: MAXIMIZING EFFICIENCY AND PERFORMANCE (continued)

KPI	SUB-METRIC	PRODUCT/ PROCESS 1 BEFORE SUSTAINABILITY TRANSFORMATION	PRODUCT/ PROCESS 2 UNEXPECTED SOLUTION: SUSTAINABLE EARTH	RATING
	Smog formation potential (in kg O emissions)			
Human health metrics	Number of restricted chemicals according to EU and US guidelines			
	Percentage of chemicals linked to high acuity, disease, and procedural complexity (i.e., high-cost patients)			
	Percentage of chemicals linked to high acuity, disease, and procedural complexity (i.e., moderately high-cost patients)			

(continued)

SCORECARD COMPONENT: MAXIMIZING EFFICIENCY AND PERFORMANCE (continued)

KPI	SUB-METRIC	PRODUCT/ PROCESS 1 BEFORE SUSTAINABILITY TRANSFORMATION	PRODUCT/ PROCESS 2 UNEXPECTED SOLUTION: SUSTAINABLE EARTH	R A T I N G
	Percentage of chemicals with robust data sources on assessment of health impacts			

- 0: process is maximally efficient and has no negative environmental or human health externalities.
- 1: process under evaluation is efficient, and the majority (51% or more) of chemicals under evaluation are not linked to high acuity and complexity disorders.
- 2: process under evaluation is efficient, and the majority (51%–90%) of chemicals under evaluation are linked to high acuity and complexity disorders.
- 3: process under evaluation is efficient, and all of the chemicals under evaluation are linked to high acuity and complexity disorders.

SCORECARD COMPONENT: USING RENEWABLE INPUTS

KPI	SUB-METRIC	PRODUCT/ PROCESS 1 BEFORE SUSTAINABILITY TRANSFORMATION	PRODUCT/ PROCESS 2 UNEXPECTED SOLUTION: SUSTAINABLE EARTH	RATING
Renewable carbon-free energy inputs	Percentage of renewable carbon			
	Percentage of carbon-negative carbon			
Waste energy utilization				
Renewable feedstocks	Percentage of total inputs that are derived from renewable resources			
Renewable freestocks	Percentage of renewable carbon			
	Percentage of carbon-negative carbon			

- 0: product under evaluation uses 90%–100% of renewable inputs in the entire known supply chain.
- 1: product under evaluation leverages renewable inputs for the majority (51%–90%) of the entire known supply chain.

- 2: product under evaluation leverages nonrenewable inputs for the majority (51%–90%) of the entire known supply chain.
- 3: product under evaluation leverages nonrenewable inputs for 100% of the entire known supply chain.

SCORECARD COMPONENT: ENSURING SAFE DEGRADATION

KPI	SUB-METRIC	PRODUCT/ PROCESS 1 BEFORE SUSTAINABILITY TRANSFORMATION	PRODUCT/ PROCESS 2 UNEXPECTED SOLUTION: SUSTAINABLE EARTH	RATING
Persistence (a measure of transgenerational design)	Percentage of "forever chemicals" in final product			
Bioaccumulation	Bioaccumulation factor			
Exposure	Induction period and duration of product life			
	Latent period and duration of product life			

- 0: process degrades without any toxic effects on human health and environmental factors *and* extended producer responsibility is in place.
- 1: process degrades without any toxic effects, but extended producer responsibility is not in place.

- 2: majority of the components of the process degrade safely, but extended producer responsibility is not in place.
- 3: process does not degrade safely (i.e., is toxic, persistent, and bioaccumulative).

The Sustainability Scorecard provides a consistent and reliable framework for measuring the comprehensive value of business processes and communicating the full life-cycle cost-benefit improvements achieved. It is built on the backbone of the four principles for managing and scaling sustainability introduced in the previous chapter and highlights the four main goals of a sustainable corporate strategy:

1. Waste prevention
2. Maximizing efficiency and performance
3. Renewable inputs
4. Safe degradation

But before diving into the specific metrics and their leading indicators (i.e., compass points), let's discuss the intention behind the scorecard.

The Intention behind the Scorecard
Uncovers Hidden Costs

Research into business practices tells us that over 70 percent of the costs of a product are budgeted in the design phase. Although the financial investment into a new product or process is typically accounted for during the design phase, most of a product's social and environmental costs are actually incurred much later in the product life cycle.[1] The Sustainability Scorecard solves a big issue for leaders in this area: the identification of costs incurred during each phase of a product's life cycle, including production, use, end of life, and disposal. Once these costs can be holistically anticipated and tracked, they can also be more effectively managed or eliminated.

Is Flexible and Customizable

This scorecard is designed to be customized. While the principles in this scorecard should be leveraged as the arms of a compass and are widely applicable across numerous industries and use cases, the exact metrics we discuss may not be. This chapter provides a set of metrics to kick off an ideation journey for organizations, but not necessarily a set that is applicable across the board. For example, if you are part of a product firm or manufacturing firm, measuring PMI (process mass index) or some form of this metric is likely very valuable and will lead you in the direction of strategic and non-risk-based metrics.[2] In the agricultural industry, the environmental impact quotient (EIQ) or process excellence index (PEI) may be a more useful metric for benchmarking the sustainability of operations. These metrics are meant to be transformed depending on several factors, including the type or category of waste your firm intends to prevent and the categories of hazards and performance that you intend to measure.[3]

Is Quantitative Yet Never Achieves Perfection

We all love achieving perfect grades on tests, but in this case, the scorecard has been designed to never achieve or "add up to" a perfect score. Rather, you may note that we broadly classify progress in four categories: 0, 1, 2, and 3. In the waste prevention guideline, 0 signifies complete recovery of all end-of-life materials; that is, all outputs of the process are reintroduced as inputs. A score of 3 signifies that no outputs are ultimately recovered as inputs, and ultimately finish the product life cycle in the grave.

The reason for this broad classification is that sustainability is a journey, a design constraint in product and process innovation, and a pillar of corporate strategy. It would be naive to imagine a world where all the environmental challenges to an industry have been resolved, while innovation continues to drive new materials, products, and processes.

We believe that there is no one company in the world that is completely aligned with all of the four Sustainability Scorecard principles simultaneously. This scorecard is designed to provide an adequate view of a firm's transformation while ensuring that knowledge gaps, implementation gaps, and future road map items are clearly communicated and visible in the scorecard, and can be addressed as a part of future plans.

Designing our scorecard for durability and relevance, while remaining mindful of the potential unknowns the future might present, was a critical consideration. Innovation presents challenges for which perfect knowledge or answers may not be present at the time; however, a compass to help you see what direction you're moving in will always be useful.

In the case of high-tech and other rapidly evolving industries that are anchored in innovation and value it highly, the next unexpected solution may produce outcomes that are not fully understood for years—perhaps decades—after its introduction. Nanotechnology is a perfect example.

As Paul testified to Congress in 2009 related to an e-waste bill, the production of a memory chip requires about six hundred times its weight in fossil fuel.[4] For comparison, the production of a car requires one to two times, and an aluminum can requires four to five times its weight in fossil fuel.[5] And many electronic products, especially older models, contain substantial quantities of hazardous substances. Older cathode-ray tubes contain between four and seven pounds of lead in each tube!

In 2003, a user group categorized and studied the environmental challenges associated with the "hockey stick" growth that electronics waste presented. Several toxic chemicals that were restricted, even at that time, were found in the leaching and discharge of e-waste.[6] The disposal and recycling of waste electronics has become an international and multidimensional issue riddled with large knowledge gaps, as researchers and industry groups work to figure out the best ways to ensure human and environmental safety while attempting to create circularity in such a complex space.

Tracks the Journey, Not Success or Failure

Ultimately, circularity occurs when all components are either utilized or managed in a way that the system inherently allows for a closed loop. Circularity is the goal because such systems are not only more resilient to vulnerabilities but more effective and efficient. You will notice that our ratings scale ranges from immaturity (3), a system wherein circularity has not been achieved, to complete recovery (0), wherein circularity has been achieved with a certain process or product. We intentionally conceived this scale to factor in the maturity of a firm's methodology while combining quantitative and qualitative assessments of the scorecard to arrive at a 360-degree view of the product or process under evaluation.

The lack or presence of a strategy for the components of a product that arrive in the graveyard along any process flow is also indicative of process maturity. A commonly used tool for assessing the "greenness" of a particular process is the life-cycle assessment (LCA). The LCA measures the environmental impact of every stage of production and post-production life of a product or service. In this assessment, the end-of-life disposal step of this product or process is called a graveyard. The lack of a strategy to address the disposal or graveyard effects of a firm's products is an indicator of process immaturity, considering that the financial benefits of material and energy-flow recovery have been well documented in various industries. Firms early in their sustainability journey typically do not have established recovery mechanisms within their product stewardship programs. In these scenarios, the relationship between the product and the firm ends at the transaction, when the product then belongs to the customer, as does responsibility for disposal. In mature processes, graveyard effects are addressed and owned by the manufacturer or firm—even after the transaction with the customer has occurred.

And where inherent design challenges persist (e.g., in the case of electronics, where the true carbon footprint of nanochip production is unknown), the Sustainability Scorecard will continue to show a baseline level of immaturity. The intention behind this mindful scaling is to foster conscientious innovation, design, and awareness of knowledge gaps, and accurate reporting.

Beyond Neutrality, Repairs Externalities

The scorecard is designed to celebrate neutrality (with complete recoverability being scored as 0)—no unintended negative externalities—but also to encourage firms to continue to innovate with unexpected solutions. Consider carbon. Carbon dioxide is a long-lived pollutant; it resides in the atmosphere for centuries. This leads to a pesky problem: even if we decarbonize our entire economy today, we would still have to contend with the environmental, human health, and financial shocks of the carbon we have emitted over the past two centuries. It is increasingly likely that we will need to employ solutions that remove and sequester carbon from the atmosphere. In this case, we wanted to make space for firms to consider not only going carbon-neutral in the future but also taking responsibility for the carbon they may have historically emitted.

Provides an Understanding of the Life-Cycle Costs and Benefits

It is important to recognize that when attempting to embed unexpected solutions into existing systems, a full cost-benefit analysis of the life cycle is the best way to compare a traditional product or process and an unexpected one. For solutions that provide value along various parameters (such as unexpected solutions), the Sustainability Scorecard will enable operations executives to see where investments can be made for product and process innovation. These powerful drivers can be harnessed to encourage behavior and decision-making that are aligned with the corporate strategic goals of the future.

Enables Full-Cost Accounting

By evaluating a process or product through the lens of this scorecard, it is possible to understand the full-cost accounting and understand the economic cost of each externality and end point (recovery or landfill), and it allows for better management of natural and social resources.

Drives New, Unexpected Solutions

Like any self-reported questionnaire, the Sustainability Scorecard can be manipulated to provide an exaggeratedly positive output. And in a competitive market environment in which being "green" is something that appeals to customers, businesses have a lot to gain by pretending to be more sustainable than they really are. However, when our scorecard elements are placed as design requirements, they can drive unexpected innovations and new product development. This can result in the creation of incentives that mitigate against the risk of overly aspirational self-assessments and reporting.

And now, let's get to the goodies. Next, we'll discuss the most universally applicable Sustainability Scorecard KPIs and how you can use them as leading indicators for your firm's progress.

Enable Strategic Sustainability Metrics

We have now discussed some of the main sustainability KPIs under each principle. These KPIs are intentionally nonreductive and forward facing.

Waste Prevention

In tracking waste prevention, there are several leading indicators or KPIs that we can use to determine whether we're moving in the direction of greater sustainability.

Durability. Products that will last well beyond their useful commercial life often result in environmental problems, ranging from solid waste disposal to persistence and bioaccumulation. It is therefore necessary to design substances with a targeted lifetime to avoid the persistence of undesirable materials in the environment, also known as "forever chemicals" that affect human health through a variety of pathways. However, there is a balancing act to be managed. We want the product to tolerate operating conditions for its expected lifetime, and we do not want it to prematurely fail—however we define failure for that category. Effective and efficient maintenance and repair must also be considered, so that the intended lifetime can be achieved with the minimal introduction of additional material and energy throughout the life cycle.

As an example, plastics consisting of several materials, including nonbiodegradable polymers, represent the second-largest nonrecyclable fraction of municipal solid waste that finds its way into landfills, surpassing every other category quite significantly.[7] Although this product has a short useful lifetime, it remains a significant source of environmental pollution by living far beyond its useful life in landfills, with plastic and fibrous components degrading into the soil and groundwater, placing humans miles away at risk.

One emerging solution is a starch-based packing material, Eco-fill, which consists of food-grade inputs (starch and water) that are durable enough to perform their function for the time period and can be dissolved in domestic or industrial water systems at the product's end of life.[8]

Whatever your product, it is important to consider the range in which durability can be withstood without designing for immortality. We don't want products that are no longer useful to live forever! And if they do, we'd advise designing for recoverability and/or safe degradation. In designing for the durability of a product, important sub-metrics to steer the way include

- Expected useful life of the product/expected number of uses before a replacement is required

- Failure frequency
- Tolerance to disturbance while remaining "viable"

Product life extension. This metric is really a component of durability. One of the approaches that firms often employ in designing their end-of-life solutions is to prolong the useful life of a product. This can be achieved in several ways—upcycling, for example. Adidas uses ocean plastic to produce its shoe. By way of leveraging a discarded product in the creation of a new one, an important cradle-to-cradle solution is born. Product life extension can also be a useful revenue-generating mechanism to ensure the prolonged life of products while diverting these products from graveyards. The sub-metrics we have identified that are most directly related to product life extension are

- Customer lifetime value
- Customer acquisition cost

As firms clean up their acts (literally), customer lifetime value has become an increasingly important metric. In the case of sustainable supply chains, this metric is the percentage spend of an account over the life of the account. Increasing the useful life of your product could mean that it is better (and cheaper) for the customer over the long term. And if the products that you are creating are inherently better and more cost-effective, it is likely that not only will customer retention increase but customer acquisition costs will decline.

While one can attempt to continually decrease customer acquisition costs over time via several strategies, customer lifetime value remains a consistently strong lever in strategic sustainable growth. In chapter 8, Roger McFadden, ex-Chief Science Officer of Coastwide Laboratories/ Corporate Express (and later VP and Senior Scientist at Staples) sheds light on just how important a sustainability progress measure customer lifetime value has been in the commercial and household cleaning supplies industry.

Process mass intensity (PMI). The PMI metric is a measure or ratio of the weights of all material inputs into a product (water, organic solvents, raw materials, reagents, process aids, etc.) in relation to the ultimate weight of the product produced. This is an important focus because of the historically large amount of waste coproduced during manufacturing.

One of the biggest successes in implementing this metric has been in the biopharmaceutical industry, which in many cases creates more than one hundred kilos of waste per kilo of product. Biopharmaceuticals, or biologics as they are commonly known, are large-molecule therapeutics typically produced using biotechnology; they form a rapidly growing segment of the pharmaceutical market.[9] Despite the success these drugs have had in treating various ailments, their hefty environmental footprint has gained significant attention in the media, with several stakeholders—healthcare providers, investors, and even employees at pharmaceutical firms—ringing the alarm.[10] At the 2012 American Chemical Society Green Chemistry Institute, six large pharmaceutical companies participated in a benchmarking exercise to calculate the PMI for drugs for monoclonal antibody (henceforth referred to as mAb) production. They found that on average, 7,700 kg of input is required to produce 1 kg of mAb. Over 90 percent of the mass is due to water use, highlighting the water-intensive nature of biologics production, and the rest is solid waste. It became clear that a focus on reducing this waste would result in significant production cost savings.[11]

With this information, Merck attempted reducing the PMI of Simvastatin, their leading cholesterol-lowering biologic, originally developed as Zocor®.[12] In 2005, Zocor was Merck's best-selling drug and the second-largest-selling statin in the world, with about $5 billion in sales. After Zocor went off patent in 2006, Simvastatin became the most-prescribed generic statin, with ninety-four million prescriptions filled in 2010.[13] Off-patent drugs face fierce competition in the marketplace, as other firms' products can compete with the drug and potentially drive down the price. With over 70 percent of waste being expended in the

traditional production of Simvastatin, Merck knew there was a fantastic opportunity to drive down the cost of production by simply using
fewer inputs, producing (and therefore managing) less waste per pill.
In 2012, Professor Yi Tang of UCLA and his team developed a new process for the production of this biologic, using less-hazardous inputs that
produce only one recyclable waste product. In addition, 97 percent of
the inputs of this process make their way into the final output, meaning that only 3 percent of the entire ingredient list has to be recycled.
With novel and cost-effective technology, more than ten metric tons of
this drug have been manufactured using this new process, and in 2012,
Tang was awarded the Presidential Green Chemistry Award for his exceptional work.[14]

Economy of space. Traditionally, manufacturing requires many
steps, especially for complex products with various inputs. For example, in pharmaceuticals, the creation of complex drugs such as antican-
cer therapeutics requires multistep processes that can result in loss of
material, low yields, and increased energy and time used. Economy of
space (i.e., fewer production sites) and economy of manufacturing steps
(in the case of pharmaceuticals, for example, "one-pot" synthesis in a
minimal number of steps or reactions) will not only decrease production costs but also lead to

- Higher yields
- Higher-quality outputs
- Increase in the number of units per square foot of product
- Increase in the number of units transported per vehicle

In the case of Zoloft, one of the most frequently prescribed
medications for depression, Pfizer dramatically improved the commercial manufacturing process for the drug by replacing a process
called sertraline. Sertraline was a three-step process in the original
manufacturing, which was replaced by a one-pot creation method
that reduced the three steps down to one. Chemically, the firm leveraged the use of a very selective catalyst to not only accelerate the

speed of drug production but also increase the yield of the desired drug. The firm focused on designing a manufacturing process that reduced production cost, improved the yield and quality of the final output, and also

- Used benign chemicals for drug production, thereby eliminating significant costs associated with the safe handling of drugs, biohazards, and worker safety. Simply reducing the manufacturing steps resulted in elimination of 310,000 pounds of toxic waste production per year. This elimination resulted both in cost savings and the avoidance of the possibility of a terrorist attack on the chemical plant that was producing and storing the toxic chemical.
- Reduced raw material use over the entire process by over 50%, further eliminating waste and reducing cost of production.

Another way to think about the economy of space is to consider business operations. During his work at Coastwide Labs, Roger McFadden considered the economy of space in product transportation. In changing the shape of product containers from a traditionally tapered conical shape to an S shape, the lab was able to fit 25 percent more product in a transportation container. When the operational savings on one container are scaled across an entire production line and considered year over year, this change yields significant financial benefits.

Maximizing Energy and Performance

Material efficiency and environmental health benefits. A gap we often see in reported metrics (in reductive metrics in general) is the ad hoc use of efficiency metrics (for example, production rate) as a one-dimensional concept. The value-add with the scorecard is that you're looking at efficiency, but it's no longer telling you only one part of the story (how efficient you are in production). It is also telling you how you use your space (particularly useful in the case of land-use metrics, such as for corn-based biofuels, where it would be clear to see that while the fuel efficiency is good, the use of land is so high that it causes local agricultural supply chains to get disrupted). Similarly, mass efficiency of a product will tell us the mass of the desired output divided by the total mass of the output—a big indicator of waste.

If a system is designed, used, or applied at less than maximum efficiency, resources are not just being wasted throughout the life cycle; the waste could also pose hazards to humans and the environment. The aim here is to view inputs alongside space, energy, and time, and mass efficiency metrics to evaluate the overall process design and eliminate waste. These metrics can also be used for real-time monitoring to ensure that optimized systems continue to operate under the intended design conditions.

For example, historically, only a part of the available volume of large-batch reactors in chemical manufacturing had been used during the reaction period, leaving significant space open. But this practice diluted the chemical reaction, making it more energy inefficient and expensive. Through process intensification techniques, such as the use of micro-reactors that operate continuously at very low volume with efficient mixing, higher productivity can be obtained from smaller amounts of material. Similarly, in the paint industry there has been a shift toward the manufacture of powdered coatings because they are more space, time, mass, and energy efficient (and therefore cheaper to produce) than liquid paint.

Nexus thinking and nexus energy efficiency. "Nexus thinking" allows us to understand the *consumption efficiency* or *nexus efficiency* of natural resources as they are leveraged to create energy. For example, the water–energy nexus is the relationship between the water used for energy production, including both electricity and sources of fuel such as oil and natural gas, and the energy consumed to extract, purify, deliver, heat/cool, treat, and dispose of water (and wastewater), sometimes referred to as the energy intensity of process.

So what is nexus thinking?

Julie Zimmerman, green engineering professor and nexus-energy expert at Yale University, explained it like this:

> Just like you talk about embedded carbon in products, we talk about embedded water. Just like you do a carbon footprint, you can talk about a water footprint of a product. How much volume of fresh water is used to produce that product over the production chain? Whether I'm growing crops and I'm harvesting them . . . and I'm processing them, how much irrigation water goes into that crop? If I'm mining, how much water am I using in that process? Or energy production, how much water am I using in fracking and how do I account for that water across the entire supply chain?[15]

In our interconnected world, energy is derived from various sources to form hybrid grids that leverage public-private partnerships. Because of this, understanding the pricing structure of energy and the nexus energy efficiency is very important: How are resources that are typically considered public goods, such as water, being used in creating energy to run processes that are private in nature, such as the production of goods? In this way, measuring nexus-energy efficiency has the power to transform energy governance, oversight, regulation, and pricing models.

Nexus thinking is highly relevant from a supply-chain perspective to address important operational strategy questions:

- Where is the embedded water in my product or process coming from? As Zimmerman mentions in her research, tracing the supply chain is effective in understanding whether an organization is drawing on water from a scarce basin or not and enables firms to manage water and other inputs in the systematic manner that fossil fuel resources are managed.
- How can organizations increase their water efficiency?

What are the water-related dependencies that production sites are inheriting by way of location of production processes in certain geographies? From the perspective of organizations, these nexus questions can address critical supply-chain and operational strategy issues that are environmental in origin. For example, if a firm is considering engaging in a strategic partnership for its agricultural supply chain with an organization in a water-scarce country, nexus questions will help the firm understand the risk of becoming water dependent and can help it pursue relationships with organizations that source goods from water-rich geographies.

When governments or organizations set goals to address energy efficiency, looking at the nexus also helps shift the focus to understand how best to invest resources to address the problem. Take California. California set audacious goals to reduce carbon emissions, and it spent tens of millions of dollars upgrading the energy grid to meet them. However, when Zimmerman conducted an analysis of how efficiently the invested dollars addressed the energy problem, she arrived at a surprising finding: addressing the state's carbon goals through water conservation instead of through upgrading the grid would have been a far cheaper and impactful strategy. So, instead of grid upgrades, she would have recommended implementation of a water use efficiency metric and water conservation. This would have resulted in a 50 percent cost savings to the state while having the same intended effect of reducing carbon emissions. Remember, carbon efficiency doesn't align singularly with the energy sector. The moral of the story? When organizations are looking to address energy efficiency, looking at the nexus helps them shift the focus to how best to invest resources to address the problem.[16]

Intrinsically resilient and safe supply chains. Global supply chains are now more interconnected and complex than ever, and supply-chain resilience (and transparency) has become a focus for global firms. Intermediate goods, or goods that come before a finished product, have risen substantially in volume and value of trade across countries globally since the 2009 recession. This metric itself highlights the complexity, fragmented nature, and interconnectedness of global supply chains and therefore the inherent risk of disruption for a variety of reasons.

Researchers state that a high number of supply-chain decisions today are based on a trade-off between efficiency and vulnerability.[17] This trade-off is visible in the list of chemicals and their frequency in creating accidents in the US, mentioned and outlined in a table later in this book. The EPA's Risk Management Planning (RMP) program was compiled to understand and learn from supply-chain accidents and the various industries in which these accidents occurred. Unfortunately, accidents related to intermediate goods, particularly those that are chemical in nature (the highest volume of traded intermediate goods, according to the OECD), are high.[18] By replacing highly volatile intermediate goods with less reactive or accident-prone ones, firms can design more resilient supply chains without compromising efficiency or increasing the operational expenses for worker safety and insurance. In the creation of circular, resilient supply chains, we echo the words of Trevor Kletz, a pioneering chemical engineering researcher, who stated, "What you don't have, you can't leak."

Paper and pulp production is one of the oldest industries in North America and reports a high incidence of accidents (e.g., chemical leaks and worker injury due to gas exposure). Optimyze®, a novel technology developed by Buckman Industries, is helping lower the industry's accident rates. This unexpected breakthrough employs an enzyme to replace a toxic chemical used in paper mills to clean contaminants from paper products prior to recycling. One mill in the United States reported reduced use of the traditional toxic chemical by six hundred thousand gallons per year by using the enzyme-based Optimyze solution, and an increase in recycling production by 6 percent (a $1 million bolster to the financial bottom line).[19]

The table shows how Optimyze performs compared to the traditional chemical.

INHERENT SUSTAINABILITY OF THE OPTIMYZE SOLUTION

	TRADITIONAL SOLUTION	UNEXPECTED SOLUTION (OPTIMYZE)
Source	Petroleum hydrocarbons	Renewable materials (fermentation)
Flammability	Flammable	Water-based, not combustible
Flashpoint	110° (44°C)	No flashpoint
Worker effects	Odors, irritation	Not noticeable
Toxicity	Can be fatal (ingestion, inhalation)	Slight irritation possible when undiluted
VOC content	100%	15%
Hazardous air pollutants	7%–8%	None detected
Aquatic toxicity	10–20 ppm	700 ppm (zebra fish)

Metrics that may serve as KPIs in the inherent safety section are

- Accidents due to intermediate-good trade
- Proportion of intermediate goods that are resilient due to "inherent safety"

Renewable Inputs

Hybrid energy systems. Biological materials, such as solar, wind, and hydro energy, are often cited as renewable inputs. Renewable resources, however, can be used in cycles with nonrenewable resources to create hybrid systems, or can be leveraged as single sources of energy to achieve sustainability.

Resource recovery. If the waste product from a process can be recovered and retains value—for example, if it can be used as an alternative feedstock or recyclable input—this too should be considered renewable from a sustainability standpoint. Examples of the use of such inputs include in the manufacture of bio-based plastics, the recovery of biomass feedstocks, and the treating of wastewater with natural ecosystems.

One promising technology for renewable inputs is algae (yes, pond scum!). The extraction of oils from this unicellular organism fulfills commercial needs. While much work is still required to bring this fuel to market, there are several reasons to consider this input as a renewable alternative to fossil fuels, especially in high-impact sectors, as we will discuss later in this book.

Algae present several advantages over fossil fuels and other biofuels: they yield more oil per pound than corn and soybeans, do not divert crops from the food supply, and can potentially be grown in sewage water and seawater without impacting the freshwater supply. In addition, breakthroughs in production allow for the use of supercritical carbon (safe and nontoxic) for one-pot reactions that save time and resources at the system level by extracting from algae only the components that are required. Supercritical carbon is a well commercialized technology in which carbon dioxide is heated and held in fluid state of matter. The precise extraction of only required components is not possible with other traditional solvents, and because supercritical carbon is a well-commercialized technology, cost savings can be realized in commercializing the biofuel refinery.

Safe Degradation

In the same way that mechanistic toxicology knowledge is essential to identify and weed out hazardous features, an understanding of the mechanisms of degradation and persistence is required to promote degradation and eliminate features that promote persistence. Described here are the metrics we recommend tracking to ensure safe degradation and prevent the unintended consequences of leaching (as is commonplace with plastics and electronic waste).

Persistence/immortality. The persistence of organic chemicals has been an important element of chemical hazard assessment for over forty years. High persistence indicates the potential for long-lasting environmental and human exposure to a chemical, exposure that is difficult to control and reverse. Immortality indicates that the chemical will persist forever.

Bioaccumulation. The longer one is exposed to a toxic chemical, the higher the rate of bioaccumulation—the buildup of related toxins in the body—in the individual.

A forward-looking approach that can be used to eliminate persistence is transgenerational design. *Transgenerational design* refers to future generations' exposure to environmental and social externalities. This is particularly relevant in products where components end in a landfill and potentially leach into groundwater, causing exposure to chemicals (such as endocrine-disrupting chemicals, as discussed later in this book) that result in human health impacts. While no formal, standardized metric for transgenerational design exists, it may be helpful to note the number of generations affected by the product's end of life.

Chemical body burden. The chemical body burden is a quantitative measure of the accumulation of chemicals in a population due to end-of-life externalities of the product. There are a few metrics that can serve as leading indicators of the chemical body burden of a product or process:

- Bioconcentration
- Bioaccumulation
- Biomagnification

Bioconcentration is the process by which toxins increase in concentration as the host of the toxin is consumed in the food chain. Because humans are at the end point of most food chains, we must consider this hazard.

Biomagnification factors can be included in the scorecard, and a value greater than 1 indicates that the concentration of the element being measured (for example, a pesticide) in the organism is greater than it is in the organism's environment.

Time and exposure. Exposures can be measured or quantified in several ways depending on the product or process under evaluation. This can be reported as the number of exposures, time duration of the exposure, and the degree or a rating of the harmful effect of the exposure.

For any product or process, we recommend creating an exposure scenario. An exposure scenario, as defined by the EPA, is a set of facts, assumptions, and inferences about how and when exposure takes place that aids the assessor in evaluating, estimating, or quantifying exposure.[20] A scenario is made up of combinations of the following:

- Sources and context of use (how the product will be manufactured, used, and disposed of)
- Environmental pathway (environmental and human health considerations based on the nature of use and on the routes of exposure [respiratory, contact exposure through the skin, etc.])

Time and exposure are important metrics to consider for any product or process, especially when persistence, bioaccumulation, and toxicity (PBTs) are tracked as well. We recommend engaging the anticipated time and exposure metrics early—that is, in the design phase of a new product or process—in order to make any design improvements or production changes that are required. Databases of existing knowledge, models that evaluate biodegradability or PBT attributes, and experimental testing are all valuable in incorporating these metrics to design strategic, forward-facing measures of success.

Consider the following design issue related to exposure. The electronics industry wants to remove a toxic flame retardant from circuit boards without sacrificing performance or function. Drop-in replacement chemicals such as tetrabromobisphenol-A (TBBA) meet the functionality requirements, but introduce other concerns in the PBT and exposure metrics of our scorecard as they relate to worker safety. Steps could therefore be taken to neutralize the harmful effects of TBBA; however, this may still introduce other chemicals that would not reduce the toxicity of the product on degradation in a landfill at the end of its life.[21] Hence, per our scorecard, while the immediate safety of the product may remain the same due to the neutralization of the harmful chemical, the end-of-life considerations would show an increase in toxicity. In this instance, a deeper redesign may be warranted to eliminate the flammability potential of the circuit board by using inherently safer mineral-based flame retardants. This would require moving away from a drop-in replacement like TBBA and sourcing mineral-based flame retardants. The ideal result would be a more favorable time/exposure ranking on our scorecard, as it would reduce or eliminate the exposure-related effects on workers and reduce the PBT impact on the environment and human health on degradation. Another redesign element to consider could be reducing the overall operating voltage of the circuit. If the voltage of the circuit board can be reduced enough without disrupting performance, the use of flame retardants could be eliminated altogether!

While exposure scenarios in and of themselves are not new, they are not routinely used in the design phase to evaluate the downstream effects of inputs. Further, exposure scenarios need to be conducted on all inputs, not just the few that are known to be harmful. We recommend leveraging toxicology and exposure software to understand the exposure related to entire material inventories. It's the only way to gain a comprehensive understanding of which inputs are hazards and should be designed out, and which ones present a low or marginal exposure over the entire useful life of the product.

Extended producer responsibility. Extended producer responsibility and product stewardship are policy frameworks in which producers are incentivized to adopt environmentally superior design, but we encourage firms to view this metric through a business lens. An indicator of extended producer responsibility can be quantified by the presence of a collection system to enable upcycling, refurbishing of devices (for resale and reentry into the revenue-generating pathway), or even collection of component parts from landfills to reenter production processes as inputs (as in the case of e-waste). We describe how to use this metric in scoring within the safe degradation component of the scorecard.

How to Use the Sustainability Scorecard
Identify a Product or Process to Evaluate

The first step in using the Sustainability Scorecard is to identify a few service lines (products) or processes within your organization as targets for evaluation. The impetus for such identification could be multifold—for example, the potential for innovation, the presence of a competitive product in the marketplace that may change the market landscape for the service line in the coming months, or elimination of "forever chemicals" from the product material mix either due to upcoming regulatory implications or to meet consumer demand.

Review the Suggested KPIs for Each Principle to Determine Which Apply

Next, we encourage you to carefully review the various KPIs we suggest for each of the four principles (waste prevention, maximizing efficiency and performance, renewable inputs, and safe degradation). This scorecard, as we mentioned earlier, is designed to be customized. It would be nearly impossible for any scorecard to broadly apply to every industry and every sector in the economy. That said, the basic premise of our KPIs is to serve as leading indicators of whether your product or process is moving in the direction of fulfilling the principle. Therefore, within waste prevention, for example, the KPIs of waste economy and space economy will likely be valuable to evaluate, while the sub-metrics may need to be changed to be more relevant to your specific firm or industry.

Assess Directionality and Identify a Target

We recommend always targeting the value 0 as a "north star." And this is where our refrain of prioritizing the compass (not the speedometer) comes in. As long as your year-over-year values are trending toward zero, we would consider this trend positively heading in the right direction (trending toward the north star). The reason is this: sustainability and material and energy science and technology are constantly evolving. There is potential for current practices to be improved on with emergence of new data and technologies. In such an event, there is potential for some line items to appear constant or even look *worse* in a year. Don't worry! As long as you are trending toward zero—that is, complete recoverability—you are progressing in the right direction, regardless of how long it's taking you. Let's use an example to illustrate. Say you are using the scorecard to assess changes you are making to a traditional fertilizer production process. You want to know how the new solution moves the needle on waste prevention—in particular, on atom economy, a sub-metric of the economy of waste KPI (see table).

ASSESSMENT OF ONE LINE ITEM IN THE SCORECARD: ATOM ECONOMY

KPI	SUB-METRIC	PRODUCT/ PROCESS 1 BEFORE SUSTAINABILITY TRANSFORMATION	PRODUCT/ PROCESS 2 UNEXPECTED SOLUTION:	RATING
Economy of waste	Atom economy (in g/mol, percentage)	75%	90%–100%	0

First, note the current value for atom economy under "Before sustainability transformation" and the potential new one under "Unexpected solution." For the sake of an example, let's say that a traditional fertilizer production process yields an atom economy of 75 percent while an unexpected solution yields a process with an atom economy of 100 percent. The trendline in this case would be upward. In each metric, the target is to arrive at a value of 0, or a net impact on human health and the environment of zero. In the case of a solution wherein atom economy is 100 percent—in other words, zero waste—this would result in a compass rating of 0 (the highest possible).

Qualify Your Findings

At the end of the quantitative analysis of the scorecard, we recommend an accompanying qualitative analysis. This is very important. Whereas traditional assessments tend to be based on quantitative metrics, qualitative assessments and metrics are equally important in the Sustainability Scorecard.

In qualifying your findings, a key concept to qualitatively assess is functionality. Functionality can be defined along a variety of parameters for a single product (fertilizer in this case). In terms of analytics, it would be challenging to report a singular value for functionality, given the variety of units possible. This reality is compounded by customer, management, and investor desires to increase the value of F as much as possible through product or process design. In other words, operational systems are designed to increase functionality per invested dollar (or invested material) as much as possible.

The implications of an F-factor rating, durability of a product, say fertilizer, and its impact on the extended producer responsibility, for example, are all components that can only be meaningfully brought into a cohesive analysis in the qualitative section. Let's consider the F-factor for fertilizer as an example. F-factor is defined as function per kg of input. In other words,

F-factor = functionality/kg of input (material or energy)

Articulating a quantitative value for F-factor is perhaps intuitive, which can be challenging.

Next consider the subsequent step in analyzing F-factor. If functionality were increased high enough and invested materials were minimized to negligible amounts (or perhaps even eliminated), we would end up with a system wherein all the function of the solution exists without the need for any invested materials!

So what does this mean for fertilizer? The following are two leapfrog solutions where "traditional" fertilizer ceases to exist:[22]

- Innovative solutions wherein bacteria can potentially be harnessed to fix nitrogen from the air and then distributed to agricultural sites via waterways (thereby eliminating the transportation of bulk solid fertilizer)
- Treating water with plasma, a gas, to produce nitrates and nitrites, which plants can use as fuel

For solutions such as this, the qualitative section with the F-factor analysis is a very effective tool for articulating the value proposition.

Although qualitative metrics may be less rigorous from a data analytics perspective, they involve integrative systems thinking (or "big-picture thinking") that is outside traditional analytical frameworks, it is possible that they are more closely linked to the interconnected nature of sustainability systems and to the goals as outlined in the United Nations Sustainable Development Goals (UNSDGs).[23] Here's how:

- Unexpected solutions such as those described throughout this book are usually able to achieve multiple goals simultaneously, in comparison to traditional solutions that align with only one major and/or a few minor problem statements. For example, a water splitting technology described in detail later in this book allows for the creation of a sustainable battery or energy storage mechanism. Another solution has the ability to utilize wastewater from sewage to produce energy. These unexpected solutions present several value propositions and can replace several traditional solutions at once. In such a scenario, big-picture thinking—such as the UNSDGs—can clearly articulate the various parameters along which the value is provided.

- Unexpected solutions further equity by solving particularly wicked problems for various industries. For example, inherently safe chemical sites prevent accidents that would ultimately affect entire geographies. Reducing social and environmental impacts and eliminating "forever chemicals" from manufacturing of everyday products have the potential to significantly reduce the total cost of care for large population subsets in healthcare and to improve the public health outcomes for vulnerable communities, all while improving financial outcomes for organizations.

Strategically Implement Unexpected Solutions to Lead to Profitability

Once the scorecard has been filled out, you have a comprehensive, science-backed assessment of how your new, unexpected product or process compares to your traditional one. This final output at the end of the book can serve as the business case for transformation, quantitatively and qualitatively articulating the benefits of the unexpected solution as well as support finance professionals in arriving at a full-cost accounting (including projected year-over-year impact on operating expenses, revenue-generating impacts, and opportunities for capturing market share).

But perhaps you haven't discovered your new, unexpected solution yet. Maybe you are still in the stage of assessing your current operations. Here's how we recommend you leverage the results of your scorecard assessment:

1. Compare year-over-year progress toward the target (0) after implementation of incremental improvements
2. Develop proactive plans to capture lost economic value at each stage through an informed full-cost accounting process
3. Use it to inform product or process redesign (more on this in chapter 5)

We developed the Sustainability Scorecard to provide organizations across all industries a path toward progress, toward an ideal future state, where economic growth and environmental and human health goals coexist and act as key growth levers for each other. For more on assessing which stage of the journey your firm is on—and how to use the Sustainability Scorecard to move to the next level—read on!

Chapter 4

Know Where You Are to Know Where You're Going

> The people who are crazy enough to think they can change the world are the ones who do.
>
> —*Steve Jobs*

What are your goals with respect to sustainability? To differentiate yourself from the competition, to lead the sustainable evolution of your industry, or to entirely transform it? More than increasing your market share, are you ready to become a market leader, or even a market shaper? Firms leading the market with respect to green initiatives, transformed supply chains, and a focus on sustainable design and innovation have different goals, timelines, and restraints from those that are just starting on this path. In our work with operations executives, we have found that firms scale most effectively when they recognize where they are in their sustainability journey—specifically, whether they are in the Initiate, Develop, or Mature stage. And, by the way, in our

sustainable vision for the future, all firms have the long-term goal of
market-shaping transformation.

We have identified a high-level set of indicators to categorize where
your firm is *currently* placed in its sustainability journey. This set of indicators, which we share in the table here, can help leaders identify

- The typical goals, scorecard outputs, and leadership strategies that firms in each stage are known for
- Key factors that firms in the next step of their sustainability
  journey typically exhibit
- Characteristics of the transformation journey that will help
  inform their road map as they progress

THE SUSTAINABILITY TRANSFORMATION MATURITY MODEL

	INITIATE	DEVELOP	MATURE
Goal	To strategically differentiate yourself from competition by leveraging unexpected, sustainable solutions to capture market share and realize value.	To continue to maximize profitability and attain a market-leading position related to ESG (environmental, social, and governance) goals.	To transform the industry and influence firms outside our sector, develop long-term relationships with all stakeholders to problem-solve, and create a pathway for continuous improvement and lifetime customer value. To create a legacy for the firm and be known for innovative solutions that will influence sustainable business practices in the next 50–100 years.

THE SUSTAINABILITY TRANSFORMATION
MATURITY MODEL (continued)

	INITIATE	DEVELOP	MATURE
Scorecard assessment output	Score a 3 in all four sections of the scorecard, along 90% or more of the line items ■ Firms in the Initiate stage of their sustainability journey will likely fulfill the "complete recoverability" status on zero to a few metrics within a guiding principle of the scorecard. ■ While energy efficiency advantages and a few other sustainability measures are leveraged more readily, the business case for a transformation on the service-line level may not have been made yet.	Score a 2 in all four sections of the scorecard, along 90% or more of the line items ■ Firms in the Develop stage of their sustainability journey will likely fulfill several metrics in their scorecard assessment for one to a few service lines. ■ Recycling and upcycling of various product components are conducted. This necessitates a landfill or grave-to-input supply chain wherein plastics, e-waste components, etc. are recycled back into the supply chain for new product development.	Score a 0 or 1 in all four sections of the scorecard, along 90% or more of the line items ■ Firms in the Mature phase of their sustainability journey are sustainable along 90% of the scorecard criteria and are actively working to achieve complete recoverability along all metrics. ■ Unexpected solutions and breakthrough innovations are integrated into operations, and operational redesign is a continuous and ongoing effort. ■ Deep and embedded relationships with competitors, leading researchers, and associations are leveraged to bring innovative solutions to market and improve enterprise-wide sustainability metrics.

(continued)

THE SUSTAINABILITY TRANSFORMATION
MATURITY MODEL (continued)

	INITIATE	DEVELOP	MATURE
	• Sustainability is co-owned by the corporate social responsibility and regulatory departments.	• The firm also typically has established partnerships—collaborative relationships with competitors and industry associations—to develop potential solutions for key sustainability focus areas. • Sustainability is driven from the finance/audit/risk departments.	• Sustainability is leveraged as a design feature and embedded within the strategy and operations function of the firm.
Leadership	• The board and upper management have adopted a risk-driven approach to sustainability that is focused on compliance with regulatory standards.	• The board and upper management are pursuing sustainability as a corporate social responsibility (CSR) measure. While the overall approach to sustainability may still be risk-driven, as can be seen	• Board communications and upper management are pursuing sustainability as a strategy and operations function. The approach is proactive, and the focus is on designing the future of the industry. Profit maximization by way of sustainability is regularly achieved and an ongoing effort.

THE SUSTAINABILITY TRANSFORMATION
MATURITY MODEL (continued)

	INITIATE	DEVELOP	MATURE
		from the materiality assessments and risk models, the firm is vocal about sustainability goals, and they are a competitive lever against peer organizations. ■ ESG factors may be audited alongside financial metrics, and sustainability reports are typically published annually.	
Operations	■ Operations are compliant with regulations; however, additional measures to compete with peers on sustainable operational goals have not yet been established.	■ Strategic integrated planning solutions for sustainability exist: life-cycle assessments and proactive demand and supply planning to incrementally improve the sustainability measures of service lines.	■ Sustainable integrated planning solutions and operational processes are focused on scorecard principles as design principles for continuous improvement.

(continued)

THE SUSTAINABILITY TRANSFORMATION
MATURITY MODEL (continued)

	INITIATE	DEVELOP	MATURE
		▪ Incentives and collaborative relationships with competitors/ industry groups and consumer groups have been aligned.	

Hazards versus Risks

Before we dive into the action plans for firms at different stages, it's important here to discuss the difference between hazards and risks. We designed the Sustainability Scorecard to take the focus *away* from risk management and *toward* hazard management—a more action-oriented, operational imperative that can be monitored, tracked, and resolved.

Risk is expressed as a percentage, a potential outcome that can be prioritized for mitigation based on the likelihood of occurrence. Hazards, by contrast, are defined as "the potential for harm (physical or mental)" and are "associated with a condition or activity that, if left uncontrolled, can result in an injury or illness," according to the Occupational Safety and Health Administration (OSHA). In practical terms, identifying hazards and eliminating or controlling them as early as possible will help prevent injuries and illnesses.

Hazards require action because if left uncontrolled, they will lead to harm. They *need* to be controlled for in a process. Reclassifying a risk as a hazard moves the actions you take into strategy and innovation, or operations and supply chain (which we'll talk about more in the next chapter). So as we move through the action items for firms in different phases, you will see an emphasis on controlling for hazards—real, harmful events—as opposed to risks, the likelihood that harm may occur.

NO ONE WAS EVER HAPPY ABOUT
DYING FROM A LOW-RISK DISEASE

Back in the 1970s, long before the existence of smartphones, Motorola primarily manufactured Quasar television sets. As legend goes, a Japanese company took over control of Motorola's Quasar factory and began implementing unexpected changes to its processes. The company set about revamping and restructuring the way factory operations ran, which ultimately resulted in one-twentieth the number of defects than were produced previously. Interestingly, there were no workforce or machinery changes or full-process redesign work. This inspired then CEO Bob Galvin to look further into the Six Sigma methodology, the clear lever creating outstanding results. That decision made Motorola a top quality and profit leader in the business world. Six Sigma was the secret to the company's success. Over the years, this methodology has not only created efficiencies at Motorola and at manufacturing firms but has also been applied globally across a variety of scenarios in business contexts, from supply chains to finance departments at a variety of firms.

The Motorola example—and the widespread popularity of Six Sigma—raises the questions: Is better management the answer to complex transformation management? And if so, can climate change also be addressed through more efficient management? Is Six Sigma or some other process improvement methodology the answer to creating more sustainable products and supply chains?

Before we answer those very important questions, let's take a moment to understand the philosophy behind Six Sigma.

A sigma, mathematically, is a standard deviation. The idea behind Six Sigma is that on achievement of process improvements equal to one standard deviation, you arrive closer to the "mean." The mean in this case translates to a standardized process or methodology wherein defects or errors are mini-mized. If your process is optimized to the fourth sigma, it would mean that at least 99.4 percent of the ultimate product is of "high quality" or meets the production goals. By progress-ing two more sigmas, you ensure that your process is working as planned approximately 99.996 percent of the time, thereby allowing for only .004 percent error rates.

Although these statements look impressive at first glance, what do these error rates actually mean when translated into results or outputs?

If one assumes a global population of seven billion humans, a sigma certification, the very highest level, could mean

One minute of unsafe drinking water every seven months

1.7 incorrect surgical procedures per week

68 wrong drug prescriptions each year

Now you're probably thinking that it's time to go beyond the six sigmas and achieve the seven- or eight-sigma quality met-rics. But the question we'd like to pose is: Is only better-quality management what we're looking for? In some cases, the conse-quences of errors are an inconvenience or an avoidable cost to the firm. However, in other use cases or scenarios, these same low-frequency events could be disastrous.

If you were the one person to have cotton left in your wound after a surgeon sewed you up or to ingest an incorrect prescription, you would consider the consequences signifi-cant. For the unlucky 3.4 individuals to acquire the "lemon" device from a production line, a likely response would not be, "Well, at least there was a low likelihood of having this occur."

In everyday situations, such as in the use of home cleaning products, even a low risk of contracting an exposure-related ail-ment is too high.

The message we are trying to convey here is not that enterprise risk management processes are unimportant. Rather, we believe they are a critical part of internal controls. Six Sigma undoubtedly helped propel Motorola to an industry-leading position and has been successfully applied across various industries in which continual process improvement is a goal. However, when it comes to sustainability and human health, no one feels relief about dying from a low-risk disease, and no one is happy about placing their children at any level of risk from microplastics in their drinking water.

Six Sigma uses reductionist metrics to optimize a process incrementally until it reaches perfection—except we never reach perfection. Although Six Sigma is intended to drive people, processes, and technology toward the north star of perfection, achieving perfection is quantitatively impossible. That doesn't work for true, strategic sustainability. The message we are trying to convey here is this:

- We don't need incremental improvements; what we need are metrics that actually *do* serve as north stars to help large enterprises reach perfection. And that's why we're so excited about the Sustainability Scorecard!
- We need *inherent sustainability*. Operational processes that pose the greatest risk to safety and business continuity are those that cause the greatest number of accidents (due either to the volatility of the chemical inputs in the supply chain or to exposure risk to humans or the planet). In Paul's book *Inherent Safety at Chemical Sites*, he gathered information through the EPA's Risk Management Planning program to reflect the number of accidents nationwide between 1994 and 2000, and the industries in which these accidents occurred.

CHEMICALS THAT MOST FREQUENTLY CREATE ACCIDENT RISKS

SUPPLY CHAIN INPUT	NUMBER OF PROCESSES	PERCENTAGE OF TOTAL
Ammonia (anhydrous)	8,343	32.5
Chlorine	4,682	18.3
Flammable mixtures	2,830	11
Propane (industrial use)	1,707	6.7
Sulfur dioxide	768	3
Ammonia (aqueous, 20% or more conc.)	519	2
Butane	482	1.9
Formaldehyde	358	1.4
Isobutane	344	1.3
Hydrogen fluoride	315	1.2
Pentane	272	1.1

SUPPLY CHAIN INPUT	NUMBER OF PROCESSES	PERCENTAGE OF TOTAL
Propylene	251	1
Methane	220	0.9
Hydrogen	205	0.8
Isopentane	201	0.8
All others	4139	16.1
TOTAL	**25636**	**100%**

Source: Paul Anastas and David Hammond, *Inherent Safety at Chemical Sites: Reducing Vulnerability to Accidents and Terrorism through Green Chemistry* (New York, NY: Elsevier, 2015).

Next consider the operational-process outlook presented above against the industry-level view, where the greatest number of high-risk processes reside.

INDUSTRY NAICS CODE AND DESCRIPTION	NUMBER OF PROCESSES	PERCENTAGE OF ALL RISK MANAGEMENT PLAN
42291 Farm Supplies Wholesalers	4,409	28.84
22131 Water Supply & Irrigation	2,059	13.47

(continued)

INDUSTRY NAICS CODE AND DESCRIPTION	NUMBER OF PROCESSES	PERCENTAGE OF ALL RISK MANAGEMENT PLAN
22132 Sewage Treatment	1,646	10.77
32411 Petroleum Refineries	1,609	10.52
325199 All Other Basic Organic Chemical Manufacturing	655	4.28
42269 Other Chemical and Allied Products Wholesalers	607	3.97
49312 Refrigerated Warehousing and Storage Facilities	549	3.59
211112 Natural Gas Liquid Extraction	533	3.49
325211 Plastics Material and Resin Manufacturing	418	2.73
325188 All Other Basic Inorganic Chemical Manufacturing	358	2.34
49313 Farm Product Warehousing	345	2.26
32511 Petrochemical Manufacturing	321	2.1
454312 Liquefied Petroleum Gas Dealers	311	2.03
11511 Support Activities for Crop Production	302	1.98

INDUSTRY NAICS CODE AND DESCRIPTION	NUMBER OF PROCESSES	PERCENTAGE OF ALL RISK MANAGEMENT PLAN
311615 Poultry Processing	253	1.65
115112 Soil Preparation, Planting, and Cultivating	207	1.35
32512 Industrial Gas Manufacturing	205	1.34
325998 All Other Miscellaneous Chemical Product Manufacturing	193	1.26
325311 Nitrogenous Fertilizer Manufacturing	159	1.04
49311 General Warehousing and Storage Facilities	151	0.99
TOTAL	**15,290**	**100**

Note that just four chemical processes and just four industries in each table, respectively, account for the majority of the accidents. This data is by no means comprehensive; however, we cite it to demonstrate the business imperative for embedding inherent sustainability as the most effective mechanism for "de-risking" or "de-hazarding," as opposed to traditional solutions that range from personal protective equipment to securitizing operational sites.

Source: Paul Anastas and David Hammond, *Inherent Safety at Chemical Sites: Reducing Vulnerability to Accidents and Terrorism through Green Chemistry* (New York, NY: Elsevier, 2015).

And . . . Action

In the next sections, you will find the steps we've identified for progressing a firm's sustainability transformation based on its current stage. Although the scorecard outputs are distinct for each stage, we have intentionally divided our recommendations into two separate action plans: one for firms in the Initiate and Develop stages and one for firms in the Mature stage.

As firms in the Initiate stage are at the beginning of their journey, they will be conducting most transformation activities for the first time. For example, an Initiate firm may use the action plan we offer here to create their first hazard inventory, identify one future sustainability pilot, and initiate board and strategic communications. Meanwhile, a firm in the Develop stage may have already performed these activities and will be using the action plan to scale their sustainability pilot to additional service lines, begin to achieve board-level buy-in for greater investment into sustainability transformations, and start to create circular stakeholder engagement, and so on. A Mature stage firm may leverage the scorecard to develop strategic industry alliances with seemingly unlikely partners to address knowledge gaps in science, develop closed-loop systems for particularly challenging material and energy flows, and the like, looking to further their existing projects, leverage the scorecard into further service lines, and deepen existing partnerships that will enable problem solving for their sustainability issues.

Action Plan for Firms in the Initiate and Develop Stages

Step 1. Assess a product, service line, or process using the Sustainability Scorecard. Firms in the Initiate and Develop stages of their sustainability transformation should first complete an assessment of each of their service lines or products to uncover all the costs and hazards associated with them.

Step 2. Conduct a hazard inventory. For all metrics that do not have a score of 0 on the scorecard, create a hazard inventory list. These hazards will range from internal, such as those impacting operations, to external, including reputation and market. Let's use electronic waste as an example. Many electronics, particularly older models, contain hazardous substances. Over 3.2 million tons of electronics enter the waste stream in the US annually, and the leaching and release of hazardous substances into the groundwater on degradation present a significant public health and toxicity hazard to consumers and populations who live near landfill disposal sites. Those who are assigned to monitor environmental hazards are likely to categorize e-waste as a substance or "material" hazard.

Step 3. Create closed-loop "unexpected" solutions based on nexus thinking. Traditional management practice involves developing a hazard response strategy, creating initiatives that address prioritized hazards, and tracking progress toward a quantitative end point. If the firm were a beverage company, for example, this could mean ensuring that as a part of water stewardship programs, blue water returned to the ground is equivalent to the groundwater extracted annually. To address the hazard of the excess e-waste, the hazard owner could decide to find an alternative material to create the device. Another option is to develop a separate plan to dispose of it or repurpose it outside the facility. However, we advise going to the next step and leveraging the nexus thinking described by Dr. Julie Zimmerman in creating closed-loop solutions.

So how can you solve the problem of this hazard instead of simply minimizing its risk? If you are redesigning a process or product, what are the solutions for your issue in the marketplace? Are there any off-the-shelf green alternatives? The problem-solving nature of creating closed-loop solutions can involve any or all of the following:

- Collaborating with strange bedfellows, such as a competitor or even a firm outside your sector.
- Upcycling component parts and leveraging recycling, parts harvesting, refurbishing and servicing pathways to achieve circularity.

- Innovating and incentivizing your entire supply chain!! This is actually one of the most effective levers in supply-chain transformation, as the story of Coastwide Labs will demonstrate in chapter 8.

- Creating sustainable drop-in replacements that do not require complete operational transformation, but can be integrated into an existing process. Drop-ins can provide several benefits from an unexpected solution without the capital and operational transformation activities that may be required to integrate a new, disruptive technology.

- For Develop stage firms that are looking to become market shapers or accelerate their journey into the Mature phase: funding a promising solution to accelerate the solution's progress from lab to commercialization and then scaling. There is a common refrain, "Who does the research decides what research gets done." Nexus thinking and creation of nexus solutions or unexpected solutions require a diversity of perspectives, competencies, and demographic factors. Taking an interdisciplinary approach, in and of itself, will alter the problem statement and therefore the solution.

Of course, there are some environmental and human health hazards for which there is not yet an immediate closed-loop solution. In those cases, firms must work to effectively manage them. The hazard response should be carried out by a designated team and carefully documented by the hazard manager, including all action items and milestones. These should be tracked and monitored by the product manager, and any significant variances from the response should be escalated to leadership.

Step 4. Pilot one transformation focused on a single product, process, or service line. Creating a single story serves to support and build a business case for future transformations across the enterprise. In chapter 8, we highlight one organization, Gundersen Health Systems, that did just that.

Step 5. Track the progress on your sustainability journey. Use the Sustainability Scorecard to track and report how your actions are leading to more sustainable processes and products. You can also use the scorecard to identify additional metrics that are of strategic and operational importance to the firm. And remember: profiting from unexpected solutions is an iterative process that requires a commitment to problem solving. As your firm continues to grow with new offerings and economic activities, we encourage you to leverage our framework and methodology to conduct iterative and real-time analysis that will enable your sustainability agendas to progress.

Action Plan for Mature Firms: Transformation

This leg of the sustainability journey is all about transformation that will yield meaningful results for the next fifty to one hundred years. While no firm is entirely sustainable, mature firms are already regularly leveraging the previous steps and are focused on market-shaping activities, rather than solely on profitability and competitive advantages.

Mature stage firms are the ones rebranding themselves and disrupting their own business models (the best way to get ahead). They are investing in initiatives and innovator hubs that are focused on placing them in a leading position in the coming fifty to one hundred years. They are looking to engage in the future *now* and create transformations that will, they hope, serve as standard practices for future generations. Their investments and sustainability pilots or trials may not all yield positive results, but their efforts provide unexpected and meaningful insights not just to their peers but to all firms. For these companies, their sustainability focus should be on strategy innovation, real-time assessment, and, beyond transforming themselves operationally, transforming the very markets in which they operate.

Consider the microchip, an element that finds its way into potentially every product service line at an electronics firm. In an analysis titled "The 1.7-Kilogram Microchip," researchers at the United Nations

University found that the weight of the inputs used to create a single two-gram microchip was as follows:[1]

Fossil fuels: 1,600 grams

Chemicals: 72 grams

Water: 32,000 grams

Gaseous inputs (mainly N_2 gas): 700 grams

The weight of the materials in the production chain of a single microchip is "hundreds, if not thousands of times greater in quantity than the quantity of materials embodied in the chip itself." In addition, microchip production is an extremely energy- and material-intensive process, and the product itself is facing unprecedented exponential growth in demand.

In an attempt to understand how market shapers faced with seemingly impossible constraints such as those described are designing a sustainable tomorrow, we turned to the executives at the global health technology firm Royal Philips N.V., often ranked by rating agencies and technical media outlets as one of the most sustainable firms in the world. That's quite a feat, as the challenges involved in creating create circular, closed-loop systems within the electronics space is formidable.

Step 1. Make sustainability a strategic priority. Organic growth is good, but strategic growth is better. It's surprising how many firms skip this step and create ad hoc areas for investment and growth. Strategy innovation involves a fundamental shift in mindset from hazard-level assessments to forward-looking goals that align with the Four Principles for Managing and Scaling Sustainability. Process-level metrics that directly tie into hazards develop compliance and provide some measure of security against hazard appetite assessments, but top-down metrics are for hacking growth. Evaluate your goals for the future and develop outcome measures and indicators that will serve as markers for positive growth in that direction.

At Philips, Harald Tepper, senior director of group sustainability and program lead for circular economy transformation; Bob Carelli, director of global environmental health and safety; and Trent Gross, director of upstream marketing, mentioned that the placement of sustainability as a core function within the company's strategy and innovation practice was key to its success thus far. The team shared with us that "in most firms, it is not unusual to find sustainability addressed as a risk function or in public policy. . . . While this organizational placement may be effective, Philips has seen greater progress through the placement of this function directly in strategy and innovation, with direct oversight by the CEO. This prevents siloed thinking and niche application." This makes sense—designing for sustainability places design constraints on innovation that can lead to unexpected transformations in operations and even in go-to-market strategies.

Step 2. Conduct real-time value assessments. Mature organizations consider their relationships with each bottom line—financial, social, and environmental—beyond the transactional. In doing so, they conduct real-time value assessments that include end-of-life considerations for their products. This is a *fundamental value extension equation* that we would like to elaborate on here. Let's use packaging as an example. When it comes to the future of packaging, it is not enough for firms to upcycle discarded plastics from the ocean. The ultimate goal should be the development of closed-loop systems by

- Developing and utilizing biodegradable packaging (environmental and social benefits)
- Influencing supply-chain providers to address their own hazards and to source responsibly (financial, social, environmental benefits)
- Collecting discarded plastics and upcycling them into new products to prevent lost economic value (financial benefit)
- Developing partnerships and scaling innovative solutions to drive down their cost (financial, social, and environmental benefits)

Step 3. Conduct full-cost accounting, the extended value proposition. Full-cost accounting from procurement to end of product life (rather than to transaction) allows for an analysis of the entire value chain. This end-to-end analysis of the entire product, all the way from supply chain and procurement to end of life, allows for maximization of financial, social, and environmental assets. Market-leading firms leverage such analysis based on product and process life cycles to identify areas for value maximization, either through the addition of revenue stream opportunities or to reclaim materials that may be lost after the useful life of the product is finished. For a firm such as Philips, this has led to partnerships that are mutually beneficial to the firm and suppliers, resulting in improved workplace safety for one million workers and 25 percent of its revenue derived from circular-economy products, which include refurbished medical devices.

Step. 4. Conduct a life-cycle cost-benefit analysis. Once you have completed the full-cost accounting, a life-cycle cost-benefit analysis can be useful in identifying the biggest-impact solutions to invest in. In other words, you can address the opportunity cost of various options in this analysis.

Harald Tepper and his team elucidate Philips's approach to real-time assessment by describing the Philips Excellence Framework. In 1891, the firm created social programs for employees—a practice that led to the creation of an environmental agenda in 1970 and sustainability transformation activities that haven't stopped since. As the firm grew globally it inherited myriad business practices and quality systems. The Philips Excellence Framework, an internal and ever-evolving alignment tool, has been imperative in creating standardization of business processes globally. Tepper and his team tell us, "This practice, and the continual iteration of our framework as our knowledge and firm grow, allows for a common platform whereby different functions can interlink. For example, in order to operationalize sustainability transformation activities, we've input sustainability-related controls into existing stage-gates of our processes. This prompts leaders to fulfill the latest sustainability requirements for our products before crossing a procedural stage-gate."

"At the end of the day," Bob Carelli shared, "sustainability operations and supply-chain transformations are about closing material and energy loops throughout the global practice. And a dynamic framework and platform allow us to perform real-time analysis and execute on real-time decisions."

When this real-time assessment was operationalized at Philips, it led to some unexpected approaches for value creation and reporting:

- Reporting. One of the metrics within the framework is for business units to report the percentage of profits that were derived from green and circular-economy products. While reusing capital equipment and reprocessed devices forms a component of the circular-economy products, much of the reporting is focused on green products that are backed by a life-cycle assessment and externally validated. Later this led to collaboration with clients to replace hardware with digital solutions where possible, to eliminate the environmental impact of net new material loops

- Creating new performance metrics. In our scorecard, we recommend expanding the definition of performance to include environmental and social factors. In light of the lack of national or global standards for sustainability reporting, Philips leadership has created their own standards, to align business and science-based performance targets to understand the firm's impact against various global warming scenarios.

- Sharpening design requirements. Philips recognizes that its products account for 97 percent of its environmental impacts (i.e., everything in the Philips portfolio outside of business travel, sites, and logistics, for which carbon offsets, investment in renewable energy sources, and other carbon-reduction methodologies have been applied). *This is important!* This very acknowledgment demonstrates an action-oriented approach driven from realistic self-assessments. The firm has created an internal sustainability framework called

EcoDesign, which outlines principles and a road map to guide the company to design 100 percent of its product introductions to meet these environmental standards, as validated by a life-cycle assessment and through external validation. For Philips, the EcoDesign framework includes the following focus areas:

a. Easy to clean, sterilize, and restore aesthetic state
b. Secure and private exchange
c. Easy to assess and track performance
d. Easy to disassemble, repair, and reassemble
e. Modular design for forward and backward compatibility
f. Standard, durable element selection
g. Sustainable material selection
h. Easy to dismantle back into pure materials

To raise the bar even higher, Philips is developing green products that meet even more stringent requirements. At the end of 2020, approximately 70 percent of revenue was attributed to green products. A natural next step for any organization looking to scale green products is the effect of volume sales on the percentage-of-revenue KPI. If these products are scaled beyond their traditional counterparts, the firm can approach 100 percent of revenue from green technology sales, simply by way of continued operations for the service line. To prevent volume sales from skewing revenue metrics from green products, Philips has created an ultra-green line called Eco-Heroes, with an aspiration to have 25 percent of its revenue attributed to these products that fulfill more stringent sustainable-design criteria.

Eco-Heroes such as the Ingenia Ambition x1.5 MR Scanner fulfill the following internal criteria:

- Meet all EcoDesign requirements applicable to new product introductions
- Meet internal circular requirements

- Outperform the relevant benchmark (competitor, regulatory, standard) and are widely perceived as sustainable champions
- Have undergone a life-cycle analysis which underpins that claim

We dove deep into Philips's real-time assessment process to demonstrate on a tactical level how market shapers leverage real-time assessments to close sustainability loops in their operations. While knowledge gaps remain for many technologically complex issues in the electronics space (e.g., cost-effective solutions for material separation and recovery with benign chemicals, safe degradation and energy-efficient material recovery for rare-earth minerals), more research will eventually provide unexpected, breakthrough solutions for 100 percent sustainable products in the electronics space in particular. However, by understanding how Mature stage firms conduct and leverage real-time self-assessments, firms can prepare themselves to integrate these breakthrough solutions once they are commercially viable.

Step 5. Draw bigger boundaries. This is where you get transformational. When optimizing a sustainable solution, consider the current design of your supply chains and products. Is there a better way? Are there opportunities for revenue with additional unexpected solutions and further process redesign?

As an example of drawing bigger boundaries, Philips executives became aware that there was no formal waste recovery process for their healthcare technology, particularly in their Africa market. This lack of a recovery process had resulted in old products being incinerated or dumped in landfills or other environmental grave-sites. To address this problem, the firm created a public-private partnership with the United Nations Environmental Program to develop collection bases throughout key geographies in Nigeria. This producer responsibility partnership, while no longer led by Philips, is scaling across Africa to create an organized network for collection bases.

Circular Stakeholder Management: Culture Transformation

Change only happens when you have enough people in influential positions on board. It is important that your priorities and related metrics tie into stakeholder imperatives and actions, as stakeholder championship will be key. Thus when you are first embarking on your sustainability journey, it is important to consider the following questions:

- **Who needs to be engaged?** What is the composition of your entire stakeholder ecosystem, and how will each role be engaged to create a "circular" communication strategy? In our experience, a good corporate communications strategy for sustainability must be circular, just like the circular changes in the economy that you are looking to drive. Therefore, communications should focus on internal marketing efforts, external communications that boldly proclaim organizational goals, and educational efforts that enable business development and consumer awareness.
  - *External.* This category includes supply-chain vendors, reporting agencies, strategic communications agencies, trade associations, and other industry bodies. At Philips, partnerships with external stakeholders—even competitors and firms outside the electronics space—have led to solutions that have optimized the recovery of products at the end of their life. Harald Tepper and Bob Carelli emphasize the importance of building a voice with coalitions. Coalitions can address industry-level barriers and result in large-scale changes that extend beyond the firm. For market shapers looking to establish best practices for the next fifty to one hundred years, creating industry-wide changes in partnership with competitors, industry groups, and supply chain vendors ensures continuous and ongoing pathways for collaboration.

- *Internal.* This group can encompass board members, executives, operational leaders, managers, and staff across the firm. Within this group, ensure the presence of sustainability sponsors to oversee successful completion of the transformation. Many firms have sustainability champions and initiatives to empower their own employees. However, such efforts can ultimately remain ineffective if they are not directly aligned with transformation efforts that drive revenue.

The Philips Sustainability Ambassador program is designed to scale environmental sustainability through the education of employees in an organization of more than eighty-one thousand people; it will focus on product stewardship and is aligned with external think tanks to close the loop on leading practices and industry application. At Philips, executives highlight that operationally, this has meant "trying to bring a high degree of clarity of vision to the middle layer of the organization." The key, Harald and his team point out, is to identify change agents throughout the organization.

Transformation efforts in sustainability rely heavily on the managers that enable day-to-day activities through their process-driven approach. This layer is where transformation efforts can get stuck, as processes and the people who manage them create embedded routines and automated solutions. Incentivizing the managers who form the middle layer of the organizational chart across all business functions is where strategy and innovation teams can play a broker role and create flexibility. This layer can be incentivized through formalized programs through which stewardship, transformation, and profitability are embedded in business processes.

From the standpoint of Board communication, we recommend creating a reporting structure for strategy and innovation such that this function has direct oversight by a CEO. This is important. For mature firms, sustainability is embedded in strategy, which receives oversight by the CEO on all the determinants of long-term value creation. Hence placing this in the direct purview of the CEO by way of strategy is important. It is when sustainability is placed under the purview of marketing, public policy, or any other department that the impact can be diminished. While these departments are important to overall firm activities, they are unable to scale sustainability holistically across a firm in the same manner that a CEO-led strategic agenda is able to effectively achieve this. At Philips, this CEO-led reporting structure is leveraged and creates an effective two-way communication related to all matters in the ESG space.

- *Customers.* Although customers are traditionally external stakeholders, we have called out this population separately to indicate a shift in the management approach for this group. In sustainability, we recommend seeing customers as partners rather than purely as users of a product. At Philips, this has led to the cocreation of unexpected solutions, such as an open conversation with Philips's suppliers to reinforce the firm's requirements for safer inputs. It turns out that suppliers are eager to satisfy consumers and find the formulation that will address consumer requirements. Harald and Bob advise, "When you ask the front-runners to communicate the change, you make yourself future proof."

- **Are all stakeholders ready to iterate?** Not all problems have a commercialized solution at the present time. Additional research may be required to close knowledge gaps, and collaborating with strange bedfellows might be required! Leaders who recognize that there is no end point in the journey are better able to manage expectations, adapt to new solutions, and implement them. Todd Cort, professor of sustainability at Yale University, recommends early communication of any potential risks, followed by the creation of an ongoing forum for continuous information sharing. The Sustainability Scorecard does not have a quantitative endpoint or quantitative target, and does not recommend creating benchmark values based on current industry best practices for any of its metrics. *That's because sustainability is an evolving journey. All stakeholders must understand that.*

What's Your End Goal?

Is your goal to create "less bad" solutions that fulfill short-term goals? To merely surpass the competition? If so, chances are that you won't experience the full spectrum of benefits that can be attained by way of sustainability transformations. You're selling yourself and your firm short.

Schools of thought around consumerism point out that materials and material products are not really consumed. The only thing consumed is their utility. Take Ford Motor Company. Sustainability firms in the automotive industry have forced Ford not only to add electric vehicles to its roster but to rebrand itself from an automotive firm to a mobility company. Its transformation is in anticipation of the big changes coming in how humans travel, the reduction of car purchases, and the use of autonomous vehicles and hybrid traveling models that are sustainable and more efficient. While this has led to the selling of utilization (for example, the car ride versus the car), Ford can take a larger stake in this market by creating closed-loop systems that maintain overall ownership of the product.

So how can you, like Ford, innovate your unsustainable product out of existence while continuing to sell its utility via a closed-loop system? Remember, inherently sustainable products not only rival traditionally manufactured products in performance but also provide greater value by way of function and service. Now that's a real, transformational end goal. And it starts with good design.

Chapter 5

How Sustainable Product Design Leads to Unexpected Solutions

The most dangerous phrase in the language is "we've always done it this way."

—*Grace Hopper*

I n designing the future, condemning the past is easy. As the saying goes, "Hindsight is 20/20." But instead of looking backward, how about looking to the future and imagining what might be needed?

The expectations placed on firms of the future are greater than ever before. They are expected not only to provide exceptional user experiences but also to design a safer future for their consumers. But the future of innovation doesn't just lie in design for functionality. It's this historical focus purely on functionality and other function-related metrics that has brought us here today. The key is instead to address functionality with a complementary focus on human health and environmental toxicity, creating a more intentional, holistic, and proactive approach to designing products, supply chains, and business operations.

An important consideration to note here is that in a systems-thinking approach, the sum of the parts does not always equal the whole. That is to say, inherently sustainable processes do not necessarily create inherently sustainable products. That's something we get asked a lot, by the way. Chemical pathways and engineering solutions may require material or energy inputs that are not always "nontoxic" in their native element. But when combined with other substances, or when processes are progressed through less energy-intensive phases, the entire system may live up to the metrics on the Sustainability Scorecard. It all goes back to intentional design at each stage of the product life cycle—something that nature does exceedingly well.

Look to Nature for Sustainable Product Design

Complex problem solving requires creativity and inspiration. One important source of inspiration for designing the future is the natural world. After 3.8 billion years, who knows better what works, what is appropriate, and, most important, what lasts?

Janine Benyus is cofounder of the Biomimicry Institute in Montana and author of the book *Biomimicry: Innovation Inspired by Nature*. The Biomimicry Institute was launched in 2006 to promote and educate the leading design thinkers of tomorrow in leveraging solutions preexisting in nature. This practice shifts the focus of designers from thinking of nature purely as a supply-chain input or physical input to an intellectual property asset or knowledge management database.

According to the Institute's website, "Biomimicry is a practice that learns from and mimics the strategies found in nature to solve human design challenges in a regenerative way." Biomimicry, as described by Benyus, lies at the intersection of biology and nature, design thinking, innovation, and technology. Most important, it offers a unique path toward unexpected solutions for sustainable innovation. In her work, Benyus has already catalogued countless examples of innovation inspired by living and nonliving organisms.

There are several firms that have applied biological system-based insights in their product redesign to create strategic sustainability advantages. The firm Mycoworks, for example, has developed a methodology for preparation of very fine mycelium, the thread-like root structure of the mushroom. This intricate structure is responsible for nutrient transfer, energy and water transfer in the vegetation under the fungus. Now, Mycoworks has created sustainable leather from mycelium, in an exclusive collaboration with luxury goods designer Hermès.

Looking to biology can provide unexpected insight into sustainable product development and supply-chain networks, including navigating complex issues in manufacturing, end-of-life considerations, and even performance measurement.

Take human waste. That's right, feces. The World Health Organization estimates that over four billion individuals lack access to toilets or are affected by the lack of a system to safely and hygienically dispose of waste.[1] According to the UN, at least 1.2 billion people worldwide are estimated to drink water that is not protected against contamination from feces, and nearly 700 million individuals globally still practice open defecation due to lack of waste disposal strategies.[2] In geographies where these issues are prevalent, childhood diarrhea is closely associated with poor hygiene and communicable disease, and is a leading cause of mortality (approximately 1.5 billion deaths of children under five per year).

Enter the iThrone.

The iThrone, a solution developed by Changewater Labs, leverages several nature-based strategies to address both the access and the sanitation-related end-of-life considerations for human feces. Its approach to "flushing" mimics plants' strategy of using evapotranspiration to pull moisture from soil, releasing it in molecular form through

PROPERTIES OF TRADITIONAL AND UNEXPECTED SOLUTIONS LEVERAGING BIO-BASED ELEMENTS

	TRADITIONAL SOLUTION 1 (BOVINE LEATHER) (KARIMJEE N.D.)	TRADITIONAL SOLUTION 2 (VEGAN LEATHER FROM HEMP)	UNEXPECTED SOLUTION
Source	Animal husbandry sector	Lamination of a PVC or polyurethane finish to a base material	Renewable materials (mushrooms)
Energy expenditure	High water consumption by the animal. Bovine leather uses 99% more energy than hemp leather, and has 78% more acidification potential for groundwater and 83% higher global warming potential than hemp leather.	High water consumption in the manufacturing phase, although the production phase of hemp is a low-water-usage phase.	Low-density material, as is preferred by in the packaging and fashion industries; demonstrates good thermal and acoustic insulation.
Worker effects	Hide preparation, tanning, and post-tanning processes use over 400 different types of chemicals that result in high production of toxic waste and	NA	Not noticeable

(continued)

PROPERTIES OF TRADITIONAL AND UNEXPECTED SOLUTIONS LEVERAGING BIO-BASED ELEMENTS (continued)

	TRADITIONAL SOLUTION 1 (BOVINE LEATHER) (KARIMJEE N.D.)	TRADITIONAL SOLUTION 2 (VEGAN LEATHER FROM HEMP)	UNEXPECTED SOLUTION
	GHG. In particular, 50% of chromium used in the tanning process is lost in wastewater.		
Toxicity	Can be fatal (ingestion, inhalation)	Low	Slight irritation possible when undiluted
VOC content	High	Medium	Low

stomata cells on their leaves. As a result, the iThrone can convert about 90 to 95 percent of human waste into pure water vapor—a clever idea, considering that approximately 95 percent of human waste is urine. Any solids that are left at the bottom of the toilet can be leveraged as fertilizer or for other uses. What's more, the iThrone also uses a pee-powered bio-battery to turn urine into electricity.

And just to emphasize that sustainability can and should be financially viable, the Gates Foundation has determined that not only does every invested dollar in toilets produce a return on investment of five dollars, but the size of the opportunity could reach approximately $6 billion in the future.[3]

From Sustainable Design to Unexpected Solutions in Three Steps

When it comes to designing solutions to complex problems, we can boil the entire process into three really simple steps:

- Redefine the problem. There is nothing more tragic than the right solution to the wrong problem.
- Reengineer. Once you have identified your constraints, it's time to design (and redesign) for these seemingly conflicting design characteristics.
- Optimize the solution. Perfect sustainability and functionality occur when the product itself no longer needs to exist.

And the results are almost never what you'd expect.

Redefine the Problem

Design is the first statement of human intention, and when we use it to re-define performance and what we want to introduce into the universe, it changes the questions we ask.

In redesigning, the first question to ask is, what are the product qualities that will hook your future audience? Don't compromise on them when developing the list of specifications.

Uncover the answers you need through a series of really good questions that challenge the preconceived notions that led to the present design. Hal Gregersen, a leading authority on creating innovative cultures at some of the most dynamic companies in the world, and director of MIT's Leadership Center, sees questions as quests. The right questions, he states repeatedly in his conference talks, writing, and tweets, take on the fundamental assumptions that everyone is holding as accepted frameworks. It's what we call finding the absurdity.

So here's one: Why are citizens in the most powerful country in the world the least likely to be able to afford getting sick?

It's a timely question for sure, as COVID-19, the latest pandemic to rock our world, has shed light on every gap, health risk, and supply-chain and economic inefficiency impacting care delivery networks in the United States. No one is safe, and most of the country cannot afford care. Let's dig further as to why and how one pharmaceutical company leveraged this absurd reality to design a good thing better.

Pneumonia, one of the many illnesses experienced by COVID-19 patients, is the second most common hospital-acquired infection in critically ill patients. The culprit is a significantly stubborn gram-negative bacteria that has become resistant to conventional antibiotics and that affects ventilated patients at an astonishingly high rate. It is expensive to treat, in part due to the high cost of producing the specific antibiotics that work against it.

When it comes to the high cost of treating pneumonia, pharmaceutical company Merck & Company recognized the absurdity and began asking some righteous questions. What they led to was the reimagination of its purification process for its antibiotic Zerbaxa. In doing so, Merck scientists were able to reduce the mass index (in simple terms, the ratio of waste to the desired product) of the drug by 75 percent and the raw material cost by 50 percent, *and* increase yields by 50 percent.[4] The new process also reduces water use by approximately 3.7 million gallons annually and energy use by 38 percent. They found the absurdity in their current reality and used it to design a more sustainable and profitable product—better for consumers and for Merck's bottom line.

It is only when you ask the right questions—or create the right problem statement—that you can generate the right solution. In fact, according to researchers at the Cradle to Cradle Innovation Institute, a nonprofit organization that supports circular-economy design-thinking activities, the greatest return on investments in design usually comes from redefining the problem, as Paul has illustrated here.

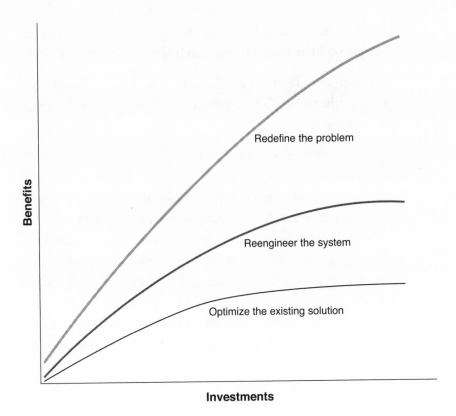

Depending on the challenge you want to solve, the articulation of the problem can differ and lead to surprisingly different results. We have found that "good" problem statements home in on a few key levers that really change the game:

- Functions rather than a specific problem
- The source of the problem, not the symptoms

A good problem statement can lead to unexpected solutions that result in breakthrough, leapfrog advances. A poor problem statement can limit the ultimate benefit of the solution. Let's take transportation as an example.

> Problem statement 1: I need my car engine to provide four miles per gallon incremental increase in mileage.

> Problem statement 2: I need to ensure access to where I want to go in the most efficient, effective, safe, and sustainable manner for myself.

The design states that arise out of each problem statement are vastly different from each other.

If I articulate the problem statement as a requirement to increase mileage by four miles per gallon, my incremental benefit for the invested FTEs (full-time equivalents) and money will be an increase in efficiency. This can be brought about through a variety of ways—for example, the use of lighter-weight materials to reduce the overall mass of the car, or perhaps incremental engine efficiencies.

The second, more effective problem statement opens us up to the domain of reengineering or redesign rather than the narrower focus of addressing incremental improvements. It might lend itself to a hybrid or fuel-cell system for energy, a change in the structure of the car for better aerodynamics, and perhaps even an ability to capture heat and energy loss for reuse.

When we redefine the problem statement as one of "access," we end up designing to meet mobility needs rather than to increase efficiency. This redefinition expands the system boundary, allowing us to think about mobility needs in a much larger context. It could result in perhaps a more effective public transportation system or an urban-planning solution in which commercial and residential spaces are placed within walking distance (or even on top of each other!).

In the first design state, you might end up with a car that meets the desired requirements, perhaps with some reduction in carbon dioxide emissions. In the second state, you might decide to eliminate automobiles entirely, resulting in the removal of automobile-related environmental impacts, denser yet smarter urban development and growth, and potential improved health outcomes from walking to and from work. You might find your way to redesigning the entire automobile industry by way of eliminating the need for an automobile—this is the way to optimal solutions, as we discuss later in the chapter.

Here's another great example that focuses on one of our biggest sustainability challenges today: the accumulation of plastics in the ocean and plastics' negative, cascading effects on marine life, human health, and the ecosystem at large.

> Problem statement 1: We need to reduce the consumption of plastics in daily life.
>
> Problem statement 2: We need to develop a more sustainable alternative to plastic.

The latter was what researchers at the Biomimicry Institute came up with in attempting to solve the problem of plastic pollution. In their research, they found that polypropylene (commonly referred to as plastic #5) is the second most produced plastic by volume and one of the main contributors to global plastic pollution. In 2018, global production was fifty-six million metric tons. In refining the problem statement, the authors found that the problem wasn't so much the consumption of plastics in daily life, but rather the lack of innovation, particularly in plastic #5. Therefore, when designers work on developing a sustainable alternative to plastic, polypropylene is a valuable, practical, high-impact place to start.

On the surface, the first problem statement, which centers on curtailing consumption, makes sense. But on analysis, there are several barriers to such an approach. What is really in our control as individuals? Is it simply a matter of mass behavioral change? Think of the number of individuals who would have to research alternatives to plastics, in every geography, through every income level, in order to create measurable and sustainable long-term change. It may be practical for some individuals, but this is not always possible and requires significant planning— another challenge to wide adoption.

That's because the role of plastics in our everyday lives cannot be understated. Plastics not only save lives but enable critical economic activities that would quite simply be far too expensive or labor intensive without them. The Macarthur Foundation, in its 2016 report titled *The New Plastics Economy: Rethinking the Future of Plastics and Catalyzing Action*, called plastics the "workhorse of the economy."[5]

Maybe, then, the problem statement shouldn't be about reducing consumption but about increasing the recycling of plastics. But this approach has significant limitations too. In our busy lives, it is challenging to recycle all the plastic we consume on a daily basis. And even if we have the energy and motivation to do so, the city where each consumer lives needs to be able to process each type of plastic. It's important to note here that plastic types #6 and #7 can't presently be recycled. Furthermore, most plastics collected for recycling in the US used to be shipped to Asian countries for recycling and further processing. But in 2019, China cut back on the import of all trash coming from the US. With few recycling plants in the US, this has left domestic consumers with a dead end to their recycling plans.

Perhaps then a strategy for managing plastic pollution is to address the operating model by which they are currently consumed. After only a one-time use, 95 percent of plastic packaging material worth approximately $80–$120 billion annually is lost to the economy.[6] When plastics are lost from the economy, they enter natural systems, depleting the value the natural environment provides to the economy and on which economic activities rely. The cost of such externalities from plastic packaging, in addition to the cost of GHG emissions from plastic production, is conservatively estimated at $40 billion annually—more than the global plastic packaging industry's profit pool, according to the MacArthur Foundation.[7]

So the "take-make-dispose" value chain of plastics may be an area ripe for innovation. And as we further refine the problem statement, another solution becomes clear: the development of a sustainable, biodegradable, and cheap-to-scale plastic alternative. It is such a simple and elegant idea—just like every great leapfrog innovation.

Reengineer

Julie Zimmerman, professor of green engineering at Yale School of the Environment, and her team advocate for the use of a tool known as the life-cycle assessment (LCA) directly in the reengineering phase, rather than later on down the path of development. We recommend using this tool in conjunction with or to inform the completion of our scorecard for accuracy of reporting.

Julie's pioneering work has not only established the fundamental framework for her field but has furthered industrial and engineering progress on designing safer chemicals and (nano)materials, novel (nano) materials for water treatment, and analyses of the water–energy nexus.[8]

The LCA, as it's commonly known to green engineers, helps us understand the real, system-wide environmental impacts of a product at each stage of its "life"—from production to manufacturing to distribution, use, and disposal. As Julie explains, the digital age we live in, with the fast pace of innovation and speed to market, often lacks a comprehensive understanding of environmental and human health impacts associated with products, processes, and technologies.[9] And according to Paul Hawken, renowned environmentalist, the amount of material used as inputs to the manufacturing process that ultimately forms the end product is 6 percent.[10] Further, 80 percent of these products are single use, which means that their end-of-life graveyard is likely a landfill. Ultimately, the entire product, from development to end of life, arrives in the graveyard.

The LCA offers a system-wide view that enables designers to ensure that the environmental impact is minimized at each stage and not simply moved from one stage to another. For example, it can help to assess whether a decrease in the impact on air quality increases the impact on waste accumulation, or whether creating a product that is recyclable ends up increasing the environmental burden in the production or manufacturing stage. Take car manufacturing, for example. If a gate-to-gate or single-component analysis of a car manufacturing process is conducted, the emission footprint that is reported may be very low. The reason for this is that the majority of emissions emitted are in the use phase of the vehicle—after customers have purchased the vehicle rather than during the manufacturing of the car. So the LCA can really help designers understand where the environmental impact is occurring and how to make decisions to improve the negative externalities of the entire system—from cradle to grave.

Julie explains that the LCA is often inaccurately used as a deterministic tool, when in fact it is a directional or decision-making tool and should be used as such early on in the design process. The advantage of this early introduction of the LCA is that it enables teams to identify future hotspots and create alternatives that reduce the overall impact of the entire system. Right at the outset, it helps you understand key questions that most major corporations today address in their risk models, such as: Worker safety—how much of the chemical will workers be exposed to during the manufacturing of the product? How much of the input will be released to the environment? And perhaps a question that draws much consumer attention: How much of the general population will be exposed to the substance, whether through water, air-quality effects, or otherwise? Does the exposure change over time, and who is affected the most—humans? or perhaps earthworms? These fate-exposure assessments can be incredibly revealing, and provide opportunities for data-driven, sustainable product and supply-chain construction. The LCA can also be linked to risk models, health metrics, and other safety data points tracked at the organizational level, making it effective from a development and operations perspective.

Currently, few firms use LCAs, especially in the product design phase. But there is a growing body of research supporting the potential of the LCA to identify the best manufacturing or supply-chain inputs for sustainability.

Optimize the Solution

Optimizing the solution requires the biggest-picture perspective of all the steps; it takes an intentionally system-level approach. That's because the resulting product or solution must fit into the entire system and cause an improvement in a multidimensional manner. In other words, this step ensures system integrity in addition to designing a better product.

Optimization of the solution occurs when the following are considered:

1. There is a desired state.
2. There is a present state.
3. There exist alternative methods for moving from point 2 to point 1.

To come up with alternative methods for achieving the desired state, designers must

1. Use all information to ask important questions about the product
   - How will the product be used?
   - How should the product be optimized? (When viewed through the system lens, you may realize that the innovative product causes some new risks or concerns to the entire system—e.g., perhaps it increases the overall energy expenditure of the entire manufacturing process, or perhaps the materials required to make the product are expensive, and cheaper alternatives are required.)
   - How should the product be recovered? (For example, have we developed end-of-life strategies to recover, upcycle, and so on?)
   - What is the ideal way to provide this service/product? What is the most effective way to provide the service/product? What is the best way to achieve durability, reliability of supply, and yet avoid immortality?
2. Consider all assumptions
   - Are there any assumptions that were left out of the initial analysis? (We want to make sure that we have

captured all the criteria that are required for the product to function with ideal performance in the system into which it will enter.)

- Is there any redundancy in the system? (Any overlaps or duplicates can typically be discarded unless they provide value along other parameters.)

3. Assess all implementation issues
   - How will degradation be handled?
   - How will end of life be handled?
   - Is everything recyclable or able to be upcycled?
   - Am I able to recover all my initial inputs and therefore fulfill a circular model, or does my end of life largely belong in the graveyard?

This is where the Sustainability Scorecard is critical, because you can use it to assess your entire system. In determining implementation issues related to a particular method or solution, look to the relevant KPIs for waste reduction, maximizing efficiency and performance, renewable inputs, and safe degradation. But optimal solutions—that is, true innovations—occur when all the benefits of the product can be achieved without the product. Consider the evolution of technology. Technologies tend to evolve in similar ways toward ideality—an ideal future state wherein all the benefits of the product can be achieved and the product itself ceases to exist in the state that we know it. (Remember the discussion about F-factor earlier in this book?) Consider the telephone. Not too far back in the past, phone lines traversed much of the landscape in most US cities and towns, carrying electronic signals that facilitated real-time communication. The concept itself was a leapfrog innovation when it arrived. Now, these telephone wires largely do not exist—unless you are watching a period drama wherein the landline serves to re-create the late 1990s. The unexpected innovation here was the cell phone. (The smartphone was incremental, replacing telephone wires and bringing the power of a laptop to consumers' fingertips.) The leapfrog innovation for decaffeinated coffee is the growth of non-GMO decaffeinated beans in Hawaii, completely eliminating the need for carcinogenic methylene fluoride to chemically decaffeinate the beans.

Less-Bad Solutions Aren't "Unexpected" Solutions

When it comes to sustainability and designing for the future, it's simply not good enough to be less bad than what came before. Consumers demand *better* and are looking to organizations to figure it out and scale.

Cosmetics, food production and distribution, sectors within consumer packaged goods, and others are homing in on sustainability as the next wave of design differentiation. Customers in this space demand products that are nontoxic, and they are educated about the supply-chain inputs and their effects on health and wellness or their local environment. But what happens when your customers don't demand it? Henry Ford has famously stated that if he had asked his customers what they wanted, they would have "asked him for a faster horse." It is said that Steve Jobs recommended that instead of asking customers what they want, "observe them, and figure out what they want before they do because people often don't know what they want until they are shown it." Strategy and innovation's design challenge today is to read things that are not yet on the page, to deliver the unexpected.

Challenge your assumptions. Look to nature. Nature has been perfecting elegant design and product development for millennia. Develop better problem statements. Reengineer from the bottom up. Set your sights on optimal—not just improved—solutions using the Sustainability Scorecard as your guide.

Chapter 6

Unexpected Opportunities for Large Corporations

"Nothing is more expensive than a missed opportunity"

—H. Jackson Brown

Change management efforts in large organizations have often been compared to turning a large ship. These efforts require approval from a lot of people, and even then may not result in the intended change.

While large publicly traded firms have a massive opportunity for impact by way of scale, they also have embedded systems, processes, capital (human and monetary), and technology. From a supply-chain perspective, globally interconnected and fragmented suppliers for every ingredient create a noisy procurement marketplace. Suppliers in particular often rely on term contracts with negotiated rates that inform their own subcontractors. Operations executives rely on the business continuity of vendor relationships and real-time tracking of supply chains to meet market demand. Uprooting or redesigning these processes is not only a massive change management effort but also hugely cost and labor intensive. Further, the embedded capital in existing pathways, processes, and products is often so well established that even when the business case for change or disruption is recognized, it's not pursued— just another way the status quo preserves itself. When viewed through this lens, sustainability and ESG factors understandably remain under the umbrella of compliance and risk management as opposed to being seen as strategic and operational differentiators.

But large organizations also have several advantages over small businesses and nimble start-ups when it comes to sustainable transformation:

> **Scale.** Large organizations can leverage existing distribution channels and customer relationships to introduce new products. They can put pressure on supplier relationships to sustainably source their inputs, negotiate rates that are favorable to them, or even create innovative financial contracts for lowering the cost of sustainable goods that are projected to enter the pipeline.

> **Financial cushion.** Large companies have enough capital to shake off failed attempts and keep on iterating. Start-ups often can make only a few big bets before they run out of money.

> **Longevity.** Large companies have longer time horizons than start-ups, which need to show short-term results to keep raising money. They can also leverage existing customers in rolling out new "better for you" products.

Considering these advantages, publicly traded firms and other large organizations can and should reasonably consider drop-in replacements and other alternatives to their existing processes to provide significant sustainability and financial upsides. For large organizations with significant embedded capital, either human or financial, pilots that rely on drop-in replacements can create a window into the opportunity of sustainability and provide leaders with a use case that can be leveraged as a business case for future transformations.

The next sections describe a few of the unexpected opportunities we have identified for a cross-section of large firms to leverage on their sustainability journeys.

Plasticizers

Plasticizers are softening agents used in a variety of products across industries to make goods more pliable, flexible, and resilient. Although they may sound like an obscure intermediate product with a niche supply-chain function, plasticizers are a huge global market, worth over $20 billion globally, and they touch almost every industry, from floor and wall coverings to wires, packaging, rubber-based goods such as tires and other consumer packaged goods, and healthcare.

The problem is that the plasticizers in production are hugely pollutive and toxic. These pollutants include endocrine-disrupting chemicals (EDCs)—xenobiotics that alter the endocrine system and consequently cause adverse health effects not only on the individuals consuming them but on their reproductive organs, affecting child development and impacting the reproductive organs of their children.[1] Yes, that is three generations of impact. It's an issue gaining significant attention from the United Nations, industry watch groups, and consumers.

There have been some movements for change, however, including a monumental public health movement encouraging governments globally to implement regulations and limit the use of these harmful chemicals, including popular plasticizers such as phthalates, bisphenol A, and brominated flame retardants. In response, the industry has developed alternatives for use on the market; however, globally there is no requirement that they use them, and these alternatives, such as bisphenol F and bisphenol S, continue to have regrettable side effects that place generations at risk.

Bernard Robaire is a professor at McGill University who specializes in pharmacology and obstetrics and gynecology. Much of his interest these days is in analyzing the economic burden of pollution and plastics on EDCs. If you wanted to understand the direct effect and burden of plastics on the future of humanity, Dr. Robaire is the person for you.

In 2017, Robaire and his team developed and published the first methodology for greening plasticizers. After utilizing a four-step process to develop and test the molecules produced on various parts of the reproductive pathway, they arrived at two chemical compounds that are ready to disrupt the toxic phthalates and serve as drop-in replacements: DOS (a succinate) and BDB (a di-benzoate).[2] These compounds can serve the same function as current plasticizers, but they are nontoxic, they biodegrade rapidly, and they are produced from renewable feedstocks across their whole life cycle.[3]

The shift to green chemicals in supply chains is a clear market trend, with one of the major drivers being consumer demand for entirely new and clean formulations. While there are varying numbers on the true market size for green plasticizers, our analysis has shown that the market opportunity in commercializing green plasticizers not only meets current investor expectations but surpasses them, due to

- High demand for green chemicals for environmentally friendly construction and in green city initiatives in major US and international urban areas
- Fluctuating fossil fuel prices and market pressures that are driving firms to reduce reliance on fossil fuels as an input in the production of plasticizers globally
- Pressure from governments and multilateral organizations such as the United Nations and World Health Organization to eliminate all EDCs from everyday products
- Increased investment from major manufacturers in the research and development of sustainable plasticizers

Healthcare

Sustainable operating rooms not only help hospitals fulfill their mission to continually advance patient health while doing no harm but also drive down the cost of healthcare, providing a greater number of people the opportunity to access lifesaving procedures.

Dr. Harriet Hopf is a professor and vice chair of the department of anesthesiology at the University of Utah and an internationally known expert in wound care and wound healing research. She and her department at the University of Utah have proven that sustainable anesthesia not only reduces the financial burden of surgery but also improves patient outcomes and public health while curtailing the shortage of lifesaving medications in the US.

Hopf described to us a common refrain in her early training: "There is no price too high to pay for infection control." "Really?" was her initial thought. "There must be a better way to control costs without impacting patient outcomes. Someone just hasn't done it yet."

Coordinating across New Haven, Connecticut; San Antonio, Texas; and Palo Alto, California, Hopf and her colleagues began a quiet revolution to "green" the practice of anesthesiology with drop-in replacements and minor changes that significantly improved her operations.

They began their work in healthcare sustainability through a simple analysis. Desflurane is an anesthetic gas with quick onset of action and rapid dispersal. Several studies tout desflurane's ability to quickly apply an appropriate depth of anesthesia and maintain molecular stability. This makes the drug ideal for upholding the effects of anesthesia during surgery. The University of Utah School of Medicine procured and utilized desflurane primarily for its low solubility. This yielded a faster wake-up time when administered as a vapor, a preference that typically costs hospitals in the United States over $14 an hour, and can result in OR expenses of over $300,000 per year.

However, this preference did not take into account the common practice of tapering the vapor anesthetic to provide rapid wake-up at the end of surgery—which nullifies the benefit of low solubility. At that point, does desflurane really provide an advantage? It was this line of thinking that prompted Hopf to question the department's use of the drug and to search for an alternative. What she and her researchers discovered was an equally effective yet significantly cheaper alternative: isoflurane.

In July 2010, Hopf and her team implemented a plan to transition over to the alternative drug, desflurane's green cousin. During this period, however, desflurane was freely available to any anesthesiologist who preferred to use this drug, and the vaporizers used to administer it were not removed from the anesthesia machines. Because anesthesiologists were not forced to use the new drug (so as to maintain the integrity of autonomy of each physician), no desflurane checks were conducted to ensure that it was not used, and no mandate to selectively use isoflurane were instituted.

The results of the initiative were staggering: through Hopf's efforts, the University of Utah experienced a reduction in usage cost of desflurane of over 50 percent in just under a year (and associated expenses related to the drugs usage)—despite a 5 percent increase in surgical volume. Second, this resulted in reduced carbon emissions by the equivalent of 76.35 million driven miles, without any impact on patient outcomes or their wake-up time. The department remained as efficient as ever.

Another change to operating room procedures made by Hopf was in the drug administration process. Medication administered in the operating room typically comes in vials that are too large for a single use, resulting in the remaining amount being discarded. The department started using prefilled syringes prepared in the hospital pharmacy; a vial prepared closest to the site of administration would not only ensure maximum potency and drug efficacy but also reduce waste. Instead of one vial per patient, the one vial now supplied vasoactive agents to a large number of providers by having been separated into ten syringes with a 10 mL dose or twenty syringes with a 5 mL dose of the drug. These prefilled syringes prepared in-house at the hospital pharmacy were not just fiscally responsible; they reduced the risk of drug-handling error by the anesthesiologist, were sterile to the highest quality, could be stored longer than a single vial, and could even be tracked by a bar-code system.

Hopf also evaluated the anesthesia workstation, particularly the waste anesthetic gases that leaked either from the ventilation system applied to the patient during surgery or those exhaled by the patient recovering from anesthesia. Research conducted at the Yale New Haven Hospital led by Dr. Jodi Sherman has quantified the significant negative environmental impact of these gases. Using a cradle-to-grave approach to model the impact of commonly used inhaled anesthetics, the study found that desflurane showed the highest amount of unaltered escape to the atmosphere. Isoflurane and sevoflurane demonstrated similar greenhouse gas (GHG) emission profiles that were significantly less than that of desflurane, while the IV drug propofol showed a minimal GHG impact nearly four orders of magnitude lower than desflurane or nitrous oxide. To combat the issue of waste gases, Hopf started recycling the gases using equipment such as Delasorb—a cryogenic condensing system that could capture the gases that escaped, liquefy them, and recycle them into water vapor, thus resulting in an eco-friendly manner of disposal.

Hopf and her team have begun to change the way anesthesia is practiced by quantifying the impact on cost, GHG production, and wake-up time from various drugs. This pioneering work has not only impacted the drug selection of anesthesiologists but has resulted in changes to the method of administration of drugs to reduce biomedical waste at the University of Utah and even in reduced water contamination by biomedical waste. Furthermore, it has reduced the cost of anesthesia to patients and, consequently, the overall cost of care. So although patients may not have been asking for greener anesthesia, these sustainable drop-in replacements are proving greatly beneficial to them, as they are reducing the burden and cost of population health programs for large health systems.

The successes demonstrated by anesthesiologists at the University of Utah are important not only for the cost and energy savings enjoyed by the hospital but because they were spearheaded by a single department. Hopf and her colleagues took matters into their own hands, documenting the inefficiencies and their negative impact, researching alternatives to the status quo, convincing others in the hospital of the benefits, collecting results and analyzing progress, and coordinating with others across the country. Healthcare professionals of all specialties should follow this example and know that if they see an opportunity for improvement, they have the power to make a difference and influence change.

Here's another example: refurbishing single-use medical devices. The US medical device industries' obsession with infection control has led to a proliferation of single-use devices that drive up the cost of care to a level that prohibits the communities that need it the most from receiving it. Further, the US healthcare sector is responsible for 9 percent of GHG emissions as well as other toxins.[4] In the United States, this results in 614,000 disability adjusted lost years annually.[5] These sick days affect firms that accommodate for employees who are unable to perform at their highest potential or unable to work due to poor health.

For the most part, materials used in invasive procedures, such as electrophysiology catheters, are designated for single use only. Catheters are high-cost medical devices and are used in huge numbers. Their design is relatively simple, however, and the devices themselves can be easily reprocessed. In fact, catheters have a long history of repeated use in hospitals outside the US.

To further make the sustainability and economic argument for refurbished medical devices, studies have found that rates for postoperative infection, use of antibiotics, and length of stay in the hospital were all exactly the same for patients using refurbished or recycled equipment, and the total cost of surgery was up to 50 percent less.[6]

One aspect of waste prevention can be managed by way of keeping materials in circulation through recovery and recycling. In the case of the medical devices industry, a solution provided by the American Refurbished Medical Devices Association presents a significant opportunity. For the medical device industry, there are a few complicating factors that affect upcycling and refurbishing medical devices at scale. Researchers

allege that original device manufacturers have driven the healthcare industry and medical devices in particular to adopt a "take-make-waste"
model so as to drive single-use behavior that maximizes short-term gains
derived from high-volume orders. One of the ways that device manu-
factures achieve this is by building in obsolescence in medical devices,
labeling devices as single use even if they can be safely reused or refurbished, or shortening the "best before" dates.[7] As Dan Vukelich, president of the Association of Medical Device Reprocessors, states: "Just
because a device is listed as single-use by device manufacturers doesn't
truly mean that it can only support one-time use. It simply means that
the manufacturer has chosen not to perform a cleaning validation."[8] In
addition, reprocessing medical devices for reuse is a strategy that has
low uptake among prescribers in the care delivery system due to a lack of
awareness. These strategies, while reducing the market's awareness of
and propensity to refurbish, result in short-term profit maximization
that ultimately impacts patient health and the environment. However,
this approach is not valid—profit maximization is not dependent on
volume sales alone or harm of any sort. In 2018, reprocessing companies in the United States, Canada, and Europe reduced hospital solid
waste by almost seventy-one hundred tons and generated cost savings
of more than $470 million for device consumers.[9]

There are several examples of reuse devices and equipment that can
be prioritized by hospitals. For example, reusable surgical gowns are typically FDA approved for seventy-five reuse cycles before they are no
longer suitable for high-level barrier protection. Multiple life-cycle
assessments have shown that reusable gowns can generate up to seven-
fold less solid waste and half the amount of global GHG emissions compared to single-use gowns. Solutions like this are an important first step;
however, they are ultimately "less bad," as they simply extend the product life without avoiding the ultimate gravesite (landfills). While such
a change will result in an improved Sustainability Scorecard output, it
is not a perfectly circular strategy that lends itself to complete recoverability of all materials.

Lars Thording is the VP of marketing and public affairs at Innovative Health, an FDA-regulated medical devices firm that supports cardiology labs in reducing the total cost of patient care through the adoption of new, cutting-edge technology. As a specialty lab, Innovative Health presents unique cardiology use cases for the financial benefit of businesses adopting refurbishing practices in the cardiology service lines—a success story that can and should be adopted across the healthcare industry. In his analysis of the equipment for atrial fibrillation (commonly known as Afib) ablation, reprocessing the devices for reuse can result in over 30 percent cost avoidance per procedure. When examined against the total number of Afib ablations in the US per year (approximately 366,000), scaled cost-avoidance savings can be extraordinary. Lars has also examined the realized and unrealized savings from such procedures. Although a portion of devices are reprocessed, Innovative Health determines that approximately 52 percent of the savings in the Afib service line alone, across the US, are as yet unrealized. In addition, the market opportunity for traditional device manufacturers to cannibalize their own single-use sales to address the demand from health systems that seek to realize this value can yield additional service lines that will compound the benefit that we see in the Afib service.

Paint Coatings

The coatings industry has been at the forefront of adopting sustainable chemistry routes. According to market research reports, the global market for environmentally friendly coatings in 2012 was estimated at $117 billion in 2018.[10] This compound annual growth rate of 5.6 is due to high demand for automotive, architectural, and packaging coatings, and from the printing industry.

Environmentally friendly or green coatings are primarily classified as radiation-curing, water-based, and high-solid materials. On application, they seal, varnish, and protect against corrosion. The progress of direct-to-metal radiation-curable corrosion protection coatings is still in its infancy due to the numerous challenges in the development of such formulations. Water-based and high-solid-content formulations are better appreciated as corrosion barrier coatings due to their low volatile organic compound (VOC) content; radiation-curable coatings are gradually making their way into the automotive sector.

Reduced Costs + Increased Market Share = A Greener Planet

The tides are changing, and the large ships are finally turning. Big business has begun to review its feedstocks, inputs, and processes with an eye toward long-term sustainability and financial benefits. Large organizations in particular are leveraging their ability to create pilots using greener drop-in replacements to their original practices and reducing productions costs. More than the guarantee of reduced costs, however, the real benefit of such pilots is perhaps the increase in market share and new customer capture that is coming from posing fewer toxic effects on human health and the environment.

Chapter 7

Unexpected Opportunities for Innovators and Start-Ups

Fight for the things you care
about, but do it in a way that will
lead others to join you.

—*Ruth Bader Ginsburg*

The biggest challenge to large organizations globally is predicted to come largely from firms that were not likely to have been around perhaps even a few decades ago. In fact, it is the firms that are launched today that will shape the social and economic field of play in the next thirty to forty years. These are the ones with the most potential to leverage the principles of green management in designing for the future.

The problems that some of the most agile firms today aim to fix are smartly designing solutions to include social and environmental goals in their corporate strategy and to use these levers to boost their fiscal performance. In this chapter, we connect cutting-edge research to economic levers and gaps in the market and show how innovative new companies are deploying greener alternatives and scaling profitably. First, let's explore the advantages start-ups have over large organizations in scaling innovative and breakthrough products:

> **Agility.** Small businesses and start-ups can move nimbly to create breakthrough products that threaten the market size and margins of competitors.
>
> **Hunger.** Large companies tend to ignore smaller business lines until it's too late to compete. This creates space for small companies to move in and create disruptive technologies that transform the industry, embed themselves in a consumer-facing manner, and even become a component of large companies' supply chains.
>
> **Upside.** Unlike founders in a start-up, employees at a large company gain little upside from the success of a new project. Their efforts could result in a new white paper or at most an industry recognition for their sustainability efforts. But start-ups have the opportunity not only to own the market but to set new standards. These firms can acquire a social following, gain recognition from important industry groups and leaders for their transformative products, and scale.

Raising Capital

Your new product may be better (and cheaper) for your customer over the long term, but how does introducing it affect the lifetime value of your customers to your business?

For large corporations conducting a sustainable supply-chain transformation, the risk of losing customers over a short-term price increase is real; however, for a start-up or a nimbler small business in the sustainability space, this Sustainability Scorecard KPI (customer lifetime value) can be your unfair advantage.

One can try in a business to minimize the customer acquisition cost, the cost of doing business, and various other operational metrics, but lifetime value remains a consistently strong lever in strategic growth. Why so? There are several levers that can drive product uptake and product innovation to influence renewed customer interest. These metrics can be manipulated through a variety of means to drive growth; however, lifetime value is patient capital. It signifies stable growth, operations, customer retention practices, high quality consistently over time, and much more. Investors highly value growth in customer lifetime value, as do CFOs of large enterprises.

In the case of sustainable products and transparent supply chains and sourcing strategies, lifetime value is baked into the business case from the ground up. You are sending a signal to your customers and your investors, loud and clear: "We care about your and your environment's health for the long term, and our relationship does not end at the transaction."

This is why agile firms such as start-ups can potentially eclipse traditional ones in obtaining funding for breakthrough products. By focusing on market size and gross margins, these firms can create enormous value, especially when there isn't a dominant market leader yet. Particularly in the sustainability space, founders will find industry spaces fragmented. As the examples below show, there is a big opportunity for small firms to capture market and create operational efficiencies and partnerships that will allow them to scale while driving down costs and increasing margins.

Ag-Tech

The agricultural technology space is ripe for sustainable innovation—especially if you're looking to nature for new innovations. Take insecticides, a product that faces many inherent challenges in development. Insecticides must be toxic to pests without major toxicity toward other organisms and must be persistent enough to protect crops in fields while remaining environmentally benign. Insects can develop resistance to insecticides, requiring the ongoing development of insecticides with new modes of action, and insecticides are traditionally produced from nonrenewable feedstocks, further increasing their environmental impact.

One firm, Vestaron, created a novel insecticide based on a peptide found in the venom of the Blue Mountains funnel-web spider. The peptide is produced by yeast fermentation, with the primary input being a commodity sugar derived from corn. It targets only specific species of insects while showing minimal to no toxicity toward humans and environmental agents such as bees and fish. Not only that—the insecticide has been approved with a zero-day pre-harvest interval and four-hour reentry time, demonstrating its low potential for harm toward handlers, consumers, and workers. In addition, this chemical biodegrades into nontoxic amino acids.

Insecticides like Vestaron's account for approximately 30 percent of the global insecticide market, and its competitors (neonicotinoids) are controversial due to their possible environmental impacts such as possible toxicity to bees.

Another opportunity in ag-tech comes from cellulosic sugars. Traditional sugar sources such as sugar and corn are expensive feedstocks for producing relatively high-volume products like fuels and chemicals. As an alternative, biotech firm Renmatix has developed a lower-cost method for deconstructing biomass into cellulosic sugars that can be used as feedstocks or as the building blocks for a multitude of renewable downstream technologies, enabling the profitable scale-up of biochemical, cellulosic ethanol, and advanced biofuels markets worldwide. Renmatix has commercialized its technology, licensing its process to convert locally available biomass into cellulosic sugars so as to allow partners and customers to build their own biorefineries.

Clean Fuel

One of the largest contributors of climate-change-related economic shocks are fossil fuels, and as Marc Tarpenning, cofounder of Tesla (who wrote the foreword to this book), rightly states, the world is still obsessed with oil. But the political and economic might of Big Oil is not the only reason the substance dominates the global energy markets. Oil entered global markets as an alternative to whale oil, which was arguably more dangerous and difficult to procure. Further, oil is an energy-dense liquid that is easy to transport; it is convenient.

But what if we could replace this environmentally hazardous source that we are quickly depleting with something more sustainable? What about biofuel?

Astaxanthin is one of the most valuable compounds that algae produce. It not only is a natural superfood and powerful antioxidant but can be used as a biofuel. In 2014, the compound was valued at $400 million, and its worth is set to boom in the future. Astaxanthin is useful to many industries, from clean cosmetics to dietary supplements and pharmaceuticals.[1] Scientists have found that this wonder compound could also serve as a promising feedstock for biomass-to-fuel processes. It has caught the attention of investors such as Craig Venter's Synthetic Genomics, Bill Gates, and Exxon Mobil as important to the future of clean fuel.

Astaxanthin presents significant benefits compared to other biofuels currently in use in the market, such as corn-based ethanol and other plant-based sources. The algae are easy to grow and highly valued as a rich source of fats and lipids, with forty times more lipids per land area than other crops such as corn and soy. In addition, Lindsay Soh, a scientist at Lafayette University, and Julie Zimmerman at Yale University have discovered a process that could make the extraction of oil from algae cheaper, faster, and greener than any other current methods in use.[2] Their process uses supercritical carbon dioxide, a "greener" substance than other chemicals that is cheaper due to the widespread industry use of this compound in everything from decaffeinating coffee to serving as an environmentally friendly dry-cleaning solution. When this supercritical carbon dioxide is applied at low temperatures to the algae, it serves as a solvent for oil that only extracts specific components from algal oil. This saves tremendous time, energy, and effort in comparison to other technology that is currently used to extract compounds based on algal oil. Scientists are now combining the processes of extracting astaxanthin and of converting it into fuel. Combining the processes into one seamless step is important in reducing production costs, and brings the technology closer to commercialization and scaling.

Fertilizer

Fertilizer production is the third-largest energy consumer of any process in the world. Undisrupted for more than 120 years, the production of ammonia, the key element in fertilizer, continues to be a highly wasteful process. It is an industry ripe for transformation.[3]

Fertilizers are produced by way of the Haber-Bosch process, created over 120 years ago by Dr. Fitz Haber. Considered a chemical engineering feat, the invention of the process allowed for commercialization of fertilizer and was a leapfrog innovation that transformed agricultural production and yield. Without the Haber-Bosch process, the global production of food would fall to two-thirds of the current level, leading to a worldwide famine.

But the Haber-Bosch process is significantly energy intensive and requires expensive technology to ensure that the reaction occurs in a timely manner. In fact, the process was deemed unscalable, until Dr. Carl Bosch introduced efficiencies that allowed for production under high temperature and pressure in specialized reactors. Since then, the Haber-Bosch process has remained largely the same.

The future of fertilizer, and the opportunity to disrupt a $116 billion global industry, lies in developing a non-Haber-Bosch process to create ammonia. This process would allow for a stable gas such as nitrogen to combine with hydrogen at room temperature in an inexpensive and sustainable way.

The key to solving this issue was to somehow split plain water into hydrogen and oxygen, so that the hydrogen, a reactive element, can readily combine with the nitrogen to create ammonia. Well, scientist Staff Sheehan, in collaboration with coauthor Paul Anastas, Robert Crabtree, and their associates, devised a way to do exactly that through a patented process called "artificial photosynthesis." With the potential of ammonia production enabled by artificial photosynthesis, disruption of the fertilizer market is within reach!

But the benefits of ammonia do not apply just to the agriculture sector. Ammonia is more than just a fertilizer; it is also a battery. It has long been established that an ammonia solid oxide fuel cell (SOFC) is not only the most efficient method for generating power but also the most sustainable. Because ammonia does not contain carbon, an ammonia cell would not release carbon dioxide when it is used as a fuel.

Waste Management

The waste management industry is currently valued at approximately $75 billion per year in the United States alone. With over twenty thousand market players and more than three thousand communities to serve on a yearly basis, the United States is on a track to fill its mere three thousand active landfill sites in eighteen years. In the US, the landfill capacity issue is a crisis situation. In addition, 20 percent of the waste that ends up in municipal landfills is food.

Food waste is not just a landfill capacity issue. It is a huge contributor to the climate change crisis. If food waste were a country, what would its national statistics look like? In size, the country would span 1.4 billion hectares—making it the second-largest country in the world after Russia. In 2012, its GDP equaled US$936 billion, comparable to the economy of the Netherlands. And with carbon dioxide and GHG emissions at 4.4 gigatons, it would be the third-largest emitter of GHG and carbon dioxide after the US and China. The country of food waste would create a carbon footprint that nearly rivals global vehicular emissions, with the largest waste footprint occurring due to consumption rather than at harvest. Considering that the per capita food waste emission impact in high-income countries is over 50 percent greater than that in low-income countries, food waste's national scorecard classifies the nation as a developed, high-income, technologically advanced nation. Also, if people lived in the country of food waste, they would consume 3,796 calories per citizen per day. If food waste were a nation, it would be thriving.

But how do the ghosts of meals past become the third-largest emitters in the world? Food waste globally amounts to roughly $680 billion in industrialized nations and $310 billion in developing nations, according to the UN Food and Agricultural Organization and can occur along any node of the consumption chain.[4] For example, in the US alone, 31 percent of the food supplied to consumers via grocery stores went uneaten; 10 percent occurs at the retail level, 21 percent at the consumer level.

Let's reflect for a moment on the absurdity of this reality. If we were to order takeout three days in a row, we might as well just save ourselves the trip to the trash can by having one meal delivered straight to the landfill.

Contrast the food waste problem with the map of food insecurity in the world, and the value of the opportunity is apparent. The UN FAO reported that in 2016, 108 million individuals worldwide were food insecure or lacked access to an adequate amount of food to pursue an active and healthy life.[5] This is a significant increase from just the year before, 2015, when the individuals in the world who were food insecure were at roughly 80 million worldwide. So while the nation of food waste is thriving at a hearty 3,796 calories per day per citizen, over a tenth of people worldwide are food insecure. Put another way, with the amount of food wasted globally, we could solve the world hunger crisis twice over.

Organix, a food waste–to–soil nutrient company, has managed to connect the problem of food waste to the solution of relieving food insecurity. However, its business model is one that anyone can leverage to serve as a blueprint for the future of the waste-to-value industry. Organix gathers organic residual material, particularly from confined animal feeding operations and municipal waste programs, and leverages its network of partnerships to create value for this waste in the areas of, for example, primary feedstocks, landscape amendments, nurseries, and erosion control. With the movement of food systems toward "hyperlocal" procurement, this model works well in developing local networks of waste suppliers and waste utilizers to create value.

Another key feature of the firm is its regenerative wastewater treatment program. The firm has a partnership with a biodynamic aerobic system that utilizes the digestive power of worms to remove up to 99 percent of the contaminants from wastewater, an investment that can reduce GHG emissions by 91 percent in local wastewater-treatment facilities. Vermifilteration, the process of leveraging earthworms to filter sewage, outperforms irrigation and drinking-water standards. Other advantages of this method over conventional methods are that there is no foul odor produced and no production of sludge, and the soil used in the filter and the compost produced after treatment can both be used as fertilizer.

Another opportunity in the waste conversion space is the unexpected opportunity in leveraging wastewater as a net energy producer. Researchers at Stanford note that wastewater is a rich source of organic content. Currently, methodologies that leverage anaerobic digestion of the organic content only capture a portion of the total potential energy possible from the sludge. In fact, the current process for digesting and cleaning wastewater is energy intensive and surpasses the energy savings in the wastewater digestion component of wastewater treatment. Researchers are looking to convert this biological waste into energy through the use of microbial fuel cells. Microbial fuel cells are novel energy conversion cells that generate electricity by taking electrons that were produced during the breakdown of organic content in wastewater and diverting them to an external circuit. Here there is an opportunity to refine the technology to generate more than 40 percent of electricity.[6]

Chemical fuel cells offer another approach here, where 50 percent of the energy is converted into electricity. In both these cases, heat lost from the process can be used to heat buildings or for any other purpose, to completely leverage every part of the chemical reaction. The promising aspect of this opportunity is the potential to use methane (CH_4), a powerful GHG with global warming potential twenty-five times that of carbon dioxide, as a renewable source of energy.

Nylon

Nylon is a durable synthetic material that when bent will quickly bounce back. Due to its resilience and resistance against abrasion and heat, the product has found many uses: as a textile; in automobiles to form parts of engine components such as bushings and bearings, for oil containers as well as in tires, and as a replacement for steel parts; and in films and coatings. It represents a $30 billion market.

However, nylon is a dated invention, appearing in its first commercially successful form in 1935. And as a thermoplastic, nylon is highly unsustainable. It is also made from petrochemicals, is nonbiodegradable, and produces nitrous oxide—a GHG that is 310 times more potent than carbon dioxide. In fact, there is no form of traditionally made nylon that is biodegradable, and it is a key culprit in microfiber and microplastic water contamination.

Enter bio-based nylon. In 2013, a bio-based chemical company located in California announced the successful production of adipic acid for use in nylon manufacturing using glucose as a feedstock or input, rather than petrochemicals. Other forms of bio-based nylon have started to use fermented plant sugars to produce a chemical called caprolactam. Global demand for caprolactam is approximately five million tons a year, the vast majority of which is used to serve as an input for the creation of bio-based nylon.

This new bio-based nylon achieved an excellent melting temperature and outperformed the petrochemical-based products in terms of having a 6 percent lower density, according to research published in the science journal *Metabolic Engineering*. The article went on to state that the bio-based nylon "holds high promise for applications in energy-friendly transportation" and "represents a milestone in industrial production."[7]

E-Waste

Lithium-ion batteries are the singular choice in a variety of industries: automotive, mobile phones, and consumer electronics. As a global industry, it is valued at nearly $130 billion. But as demand for lithium-ion batteries increases, so does their impact on the planet and their importance as a focus area for cleaning up e-waste.

Although lithium-ion batteries are recyclable, globally less than 1 percent are recycled. However, the economic value and business case for reclaiming the minerals in the lithium-ion battery is clear. Cobalt and nickel, elements that together represent over 50 percent of the battery's cost, are valued at more than $27,000 and $12,000 per ton respectively. In fact, the concentration of these metals, along with others such as manganese, are often higher in the batteries than they are in natural ores. In essence, mining discarded batteries would result in a higher yield of these precious metals than their extraction through traditional mining activities. In addition to the clear economic benefit of recycling, recovery of these metals from landfills would also reduce the health risk to surrounding communities where the metals leach into the groundwater.

There are a few reasons why recycling lithium-ion batteries is not yet a universally well-established process. Industry experts state that manufacturers have traditionally focused on prolonging the life of the battery, increasing its charge capacity and even lowering the cost of production, but much potential for technological advancement remains in the area of improving recyclability. The batteries that do get recycled are typically put through a high-temperature, high-pressure process, after which the lithium is extracted or reclaimed. This process is expensive and complex, considering that the batteries are packed alongside sensors, circuitry, and other elements from which the metals must be separated. For this reason, lithium-ion recycling remains a relatively energy intensive and expensive process undertaken mostly by academic and government-funded research centers that are looking for breakthrough processes in waste recovery.

But as the burden of aging devices continues to mount, the focus has returned to the recyclability of these batteries. A breakthrough innovation in this area leverages the compound limonene found in the orange peel.[8] During the traditional, energy-intensive process of melting and extracting cobalt and other metals, lithium batteries are treated with harsh chemicals. Scientists at Nanyang Technological University used orange peels instead of the acids and hydrogen peroxide and mixed them with citric acid. This concoction avoided the use of harsh, toxic chemicals and was able to extract 90 percent of the lithium, cobalt, nickel, and manganese from within the batteries.[9] Further, the team was able to construct entirely new batteries out of the recovered metals, which performed on par with their original counterparts.

Greenhouse Gas Emissions

Closing the carbon cycle by utilizing carbon dioxide as a feedstock or input has long been identified as an ideal pathway to the elimination of this GHG from the atmosphere and a key step toward a carbon-free future. Once carbon dioxide is extracted from the environment, it can be used as a fuel or feedstock for the creation of any number of products that typically use fossil fuels as an energy source. This means that carbon dioxide conversion is a huge opportunity for a wide range of industries, including plastics, plasticizers, fertilizers . . . and vodka.

New York–based Air Company has created the first-ever carbon-negative vodka—meaning that its production removes more carbon dioxide than it generates! The cofounders of the company developed a partnership with manufacturing plants and ethanol factories to capture their carbon dioxide waste. They then use electrical energy to convert the carbon dioxide into ethanol, a form of alcohol. Called electrochemical conversion, the process has been around for decades; however, Air Company was the first to apply the technique toward large-scale production and to use life-cycle analysis to validate the vodka's carbon negativity. For its patented technology, Air Company won $20 million from the coveted NRG COSIA Carbon XPRIZE, which awards funds to companies that convert the most carbon dioxide into products with the highest value.

This elegant, carbon-negative design has applications in various products—from hand sanitizers for disinfection of hospitals, to clean beauty products, to household products such as paints and cleaning products, to preservatives for food. At the height of the COVID-19 pandemic, the company shifted more of its production to hand sanitizer, producing more than two thousand bottles of carbon-negative hand sanitizer per week.

Disruptive Innovation + Strategic Investment = A Greener Future

Start-ups and investors are looking to disrupt existing processes and find the next big idea. The sustainability-minded opportunities presented in this chapter are some of the biggest ideas that either await commercialization or will present widespread opportunities for investment upon scaling. We believe there is an unprecedented opportunity in the sustainability space to leverage market currents *and* create market-shaping products for the consumer of the future. What is more, the Sustainability Scorecard provides a simple and flexible way to valuate these opportunities for strategic investment, including the sustainability of their supply chains. We see farm-to-table supply chains as the ultimate differentiator, as we discuss in the next chapter.

Chapter 8

Scaling a Green Organization

O perational transformations are becoming a significant differentiator and value generator for businesses. And customers are taking note.

In the "good old days," supply chains and sourcing departments were primarily focused on cost; when less plastic is used in packing and the overall mass of the end product is reduced, the cost of the good is reduced. Sourcing models were refined to understand all the inputs—including the fossil fuel inputs that were used to create the plastic—to ultimately arrive at an optimal manufacturing price of the good. Consumer packaged goods (CPG) firms tracked fuel prices. Fabric firms tracked fuel prices. Every product firm tracked oil, and every service-oriented firm that relied on the products generated tracked oil prices. The oil prices would in turn affect upstream sourcing professionals who would price the product, and package engineers would redesign the bottles, design closures, remove dyes, and simplify labels to ultimately arrive at the predetermined price of the good. Today, supply-chain management is more strategic, albeit involving significant financial due diligence. But customer perception and market sentiment also play important roles in supply-chain due diligence:

> From which firms are we sourcing our materials, and from where? What are their labor practices and their market reputation?

> What chemical formulations inform the ingredient list? Should we request that our suppliers use a more sustainable alternative even if the formulation is considered safe with minimal toxicity effects?"

Customer demand has placed significant pressure on firms to look beyond cost-based pricing, by demanding better, more sustainable products at a lower price. It is no longer enough to fulfill price points; the target audience of each product in the market demands affordability, effectiveness, efficiency, and sustainability. In collaboration with the IBM Institute for Business Value, the National Retail Federation reports that nearly 70 percent of consumers surveyed would pay a premium of 35 percent for a sustainable or eco-friendly product, and nearly six in ten consumers are willing to change their purchasing habits in order to support the planet.[1] The report goes further to establish two groups of consumers: the value-driven ones (who want good value for their money) and the purpose-driven ones, who purchase products from firms that demonstrate their values.

Customers truly have the ear of large corporations today, so much so that manufacturers are known to have hotlines to address customer feedback and questions related to safer alternatives. Sustainable practices have made a business case for themselves in the consumer and corporate worlds, and appear as line items in financial due diligence reports. However, large corporations and small to midsize businesses have a bigger challenge in embedding and sustaining sustainable practices. And the challenge doesn't lie in the "why" but in the "how."

Farm-to-Table Supply Chains Are Here to Stay

There is no greater opportunity and challenge facing established, matrixed, and globally interconnected firms today than sustainability. At the Yale School of Management, Jeffery Sonnenfeld and Daniel Esty state that the curtain has finally come down on regulation-driven compliance behavior related to sustainability.[2] We need incentive-driven programs that promote sustainability, a forward-facing approach for integrating sustainability into corporate strategy, and a way to embed "green" and "value and values" into product specs. We need to meet our customers where they are—and the customers have spoken. The consequences of not doing this are well known, and for every giant that has gotten outmaneuvered in the marketplace, there is an innovative and nimbler firm that will match its audience's desires and deliver.

However, as every business executive understands, creating a fundamental shift or managing change of this scale is daunting, and there are some real challenges in the way.

To answer the "how" of embedding and sustaining sustainable practices, we recommend a three-pronged approach:

1. Engage your stakeholders and lead with values
2. Run a pilot . . . one service line's supply chain at a time
3. Scale the success story

Engage Your Stakeholders and Lead with Values

During a visit to the NASA space center in 1962, President John F. Kennedy noticed a janitor carrying a broom. He interrupted his tour, walked over to the man and said, "Hi, I'm

Jack Kennedy. What are you doing?"

"Well, Mr. President," the janitor responded, "I'm helping put a man on the moon."

—cited by Mark Zuckerberg at the 2017 Harvard University Commencement

In 2008, *TIME* magazine named thin-film solar panels the best invention of the year,[3] and even though solar was still considered a niche player in the energy market, Dr. Jeff Thompson, CEO of Gundersen Health Systems, a large academic hospital in Lacrosse, Wisconsin, installed them in his home to reduce his personal energy footprint. At the time, solar power cost over $4 per watt, significantly higher than traditional energy costs, but it was important to Jeff that his home derive energy from a renewable source. His friends, who had clearly not yet bought into the use of solar panels, jokingly asked, "So, Jeff, what's your return on investment on that thing?" Thompson simply replied, "It will provide an ROI one day, however on the first day I felt better about reducing pollution and improving health." Jeff was an early adopter, and while he hadn't experienced the financial benefit of the technology at the time, it was important to him that he demonstrate his values and personal commitment to human and environmental wellness through this individual action. Sure enough, solar took off, and, as any technology scales, it drives down the price. In the first quarter of 2017, the cost of solar power had dropped to $2.80 Wdc (watts direct current) for the residential sector and $1.85 Wdc for the commercial sector.

Thompson was committed to doing his part to further renewable energy initiatives, gladly taking on the role of early adopter. And his investment in solar paid off—just as it did when he once again led with his values to create sustainable change in the world of healthcare, motivating his stakeholders to do the same.

Thompson served as the executive vice president of Gundersen Health Systems, a nonprofit group of hospitals in Wisconsin, from 1996 to 2001, before moving up as its CEO for an additional fourteen years. During his tenure, Gundersen was awarded Healthgrades' America's 50 Best Hospitals Award from 2012 to 2016 and was named the White House Champion for Change in 2013, among several other accolades. In 2014, Gundersen Health Systems became the first hospital in the United States to become energy independent—that is, the system produced more energy than it required to operate. Gundersen's trajectory from a mission-driven regional hospital to a national champion for sustainability and population health was not an accident, and the hospital's leadership under the guidance of Thompson took significant strategic steps to establish that pioneering trajectory.

Prior to the launch of the energy efficiency program, Thompson reviewed the financial statements of the hospital with his leadership team, and noticed the rising operating costs of running the nonprofit academic hospital system over the previous decade. In 2007, the energy costs of operating the hospital system alone hovered at approximately $5 million, and were set to increase at the alarming rate of $300,000 per year. As his leadership team considered various areas where costs could be managed while maintaining patient outcomes, Thompson took a more holistic approach to hospital management. He began to consider which initiatives in the next year would not only benefit the financial health of the organization but also improve the environmental and therefore physical health of the community. The community that the Gundersen Hospital serves is diverse and faces significant challenges in community and population health related to high-risk diseases such as hypertension, diabetes, and obesity, and other significant complicating health issues.

In February 2008, Gundersen Health Systems rolled out their first ambitious initiative to achieve net-zero-energy performance on a district-wide scale. Energy efficiency was a strategic priority in their road map to greater sustainability. With cost savings well documented for organizations around the world, the business case was clear, and the team was excited about the potential free cash flow to leverage in other initiatives.

First, they aimed to gain energy efficiency within existing buildings through retrofits and adoption of energy-efficient strategies for new construction. In the retrofitting strategy, the hospital evaluated the efficiency of HVAC systems, lighting, plumbing, and other systems that Thompson and his team had identified as "energy-sucking monsters."

Next in its strategy to improve efficiency, Gundersen invested in renewable energy from a variety of sources—such as biomass and biogas plants and later on, in photovoltaic cells. And on October 14, 2014, Gundersen became the first hospital in the US to offset all its fossil fuel use with locally generated renewable energy. Eric Bradshaw, Gundersen's director of environmental compliance leveraged efficiencies in renewables to create wins in other areas: the biomass boiler that powered the geothermal system also sterilized infectious waste to markedly reduce the cost of disposal. Gundersen's $2 million one-time expenditure on this project translated to a $1.2 million annual reduction in costs for the hospital system, and compounded year-over-year savings that far surpassed the installation costs. Old buildings such as the Gundersen Prairie du Chien Clinic in Wisconsin, a clinic constructed in 1958, broke even on their energy-project expenses in 1.5 years; the clinic now saves 35 percent of its pre-retrofit energy bill. When Gundersen builds a new clinic now the solar panels and the geothermal battery to help decrease peak usage are not discussed as separate items at the board. Rather they are just part of the "business as usual" processes.

Considering that Gundersen is the largest employer in the area, the public health benefit of the energy expense reduction was visible in air-quality improvements in the local hospital service, including a 93 percent reduction in CO_2 ppm, an 80 percent drop in nitrous gases, and a 91 percent decline in particulate matter between 2008 and 2015. The health system went further to utilize savings from this first initiative to invest in sustainability programs that address biomedical and food waste. It has even utilized the by-products of the biogas digester plant to create its own line of organic potting mix in Middleton, Wisconsin, generating an additional revenue stream that further improves the environmental footprint of the hospital.

Gundersen's pilot was so successful because it engaged stakeholders at every level to become embedded in the mission of the hospital and to approach future engagements with a triple-bottom-line approach: profits, people, planet. Dr. Thompson mentions that people were engaged for reasons other than their paycheck: the success is attributed to engagement in improving their community and patients' health and wellness.

At the employee level. When Gundersen's in-house pharmaceutical waste program was created in 2009, the organization was spending $151,000 per year disposing of pharmaceutical waste. Through comprehensive measures and teamwork, Gundersen spent less than $10,000 on hazardous waste disposal in 2015. In addition, 345 pounds of controlled pharmaceutical waste was diverted from the sewer system in the first six months. These metrics were motivating to employees, who could see the effects of the program in their organization and also in their local community. "Doing good" as a part of their work and seeing the wins their hospital made in terms of community health and improved air quality made the employees feel good about the work they were doing. The janitors began arriving early, and the engineers would check in on their bioreactor plants at 3 a.m. because they were excited to see these innovations work. People gained a lot more momentum behind the business development and creation of partnerships with the city and other public entities.

At the leadership level. "I am constantly asked how we did it," Thompson told us. "For all the projects, the most important aspect was to get buy-in from key stakeholders, whether that is the investors, donors, clinicians, or local and national government officials. The organization was asked many, many times why they were moving in a more environmentally sound direction." At times like this, Jeff first and foremost indicated that the mission of the health system was to improve the health and well-being of the community. "I showed them the 60 percent return on energy conservation investment and improved patient outcomes. There was no counterargument of any better investment."

At the community level. Gundersen Systems produces so much energy, they on occasion supply it back to the grid to power homes and businesses in the county. The feedstock for this energy is derived from landfills of degrading waste that release about three hundred cubic feet of methane per minute. Another renewable input utilized by the health system is cow dung to power the biogas plant. Both of these projects engaged local farmers and landfill site owners to strategically turn supply-chain waste into energy. Through relationships with the city council and local community, the hospital reinvigorated health programs and launched drives to clean up neighborhoods and restore buildings. Partnerships with the local school districts and private universities not only expanded their public health programs but also provided nutrition counseling. At every level, the community was engaged in the sustainability program of the hospital.

Beyond ROI, the key to creating a sustainable enterprise is to develop a closed-loop cultural system, and this happens only when everyone the business ecosystem touches is inspired by the mission. It is, as Thompson reflects, "the only way people look beyond metrics and key performance measures. The only way to ensure regenerative ideas and process improvements occur continually is to engage the ecosystem—your community, your employees, and your leadership. It is absolutely the only reason someone wakes at a 3 a.m. to check on the mechanics of a new system when no one is watching."

Run a Pilot

In 2009, Staples bought Coastwide Laboratories, a national leader in safe cleaning products. Coastwide, a midsize firm located in the northwestern US, had developed a strong market reputation for its sustainable, green chemistry–based cleaning solutions. Interestingly, these cleaning products, known as the Sustainable Earth® line, had originated as an experimental, pilot service line, which due to its rapid growth and success, had led to a firm-wide transformation to green cleaning products and a later acquisition by Staples.

Founded in the 1980s, Coastwide had become a large manufacturer of commercial cleaning chemicals and a distributor of sanitary maintenance supplies. In 2006, more than three decades later, the firm was poised to do what no other commercial cleaning supply company had ever attempted: convert its entire line of chemical cleaners to "green chemistry" formulations designed to reduce or eliminate the use and generation of hazardous chemical substances. Executive vice president of Coastwide Laboratories, John Martilla, with the support of Grant Watkinson, president; Roger McFadden, vice president of product development and technical services; Jim Evans, vice president of sales and marketing; and Rick Woodward, director of corporate sustainability, all held themselves accountable for the challenge of making the Sustainable Earth line a success. And it worked out for them. Sustainable Earth catapulted Coastwide Laboratories to sustainability fame as the first green product manufacturer in the US, with all its products being certified through the EPA's Design for the Environment (DfE) and Safer Choice Certifications. Here's how they did it.

Coastwide reported revenues of approximately $13.6 million in 2004, with the majority of its revenue coming from the distribution and manufacture of cleaning products. Of this $13.6 million, approximately $6 million was attributed to the firm's private-label chemical sales. At the time, the average sanitary/janitorial product firm was valued at approximately $4 million.

Roger McFadden, VP of product development and technical services at Coastwide, was approached by a healthcare system after its hospitals failed a system-wide audit related to its cleaning products. This request was an indicator of other national trends pointing toward increased consumer demand for safer cleaning products. The janitorial industry was experiencing a high workforce turnover of approximately 150 to 200 percent, and the Department of Labor was reporting rising claims related to chemical related injuries. It estimated that the direct cost of hazardous cleaning materials to the industry was approximately

$615 million in 2004. For a low-margin consumer product industry, these costs were significant; they drove the business case for a move to environmentally benign and nontoxic cleaning products. Applying the green chemistry principles developed by Paul and John Warner, Roger's team developed the Sustainable Earth® portfolio of green, high-performance cleaning products line as a pilot.

Scale the Success Story

Although the products Coastwide created were pathbreaking, the firm faced challenges from customers and suppliers in scaling the adoption of its new line. Consumers were challenged to pay more for the same product, and suppliers were inconsistent in their commitment to supplying the firm with green chemicals. They didn't see the upside, as the traditional chemicals they supplied were pervasive and penetrated well into the marketplace, despite their well-known toxic side effects.

Here are the levers Coastwide pulled to scale its sustainable service lines:

Innovate in other areas to keep costs down. Coastwide had made a commitment to customers to stay competitive as a "lowest-total-cost provider." The increased production cost of the new products resulted in a challenge, as this higher cost could not be passed on to the customer. In this case, Roger heavily formulated highly concentrated cleaning solutions. Higher-concentrated cleaning products provided end users with a lower in-use dilution cost. Ultimately, the Sustainable Earth® products were high performance, safer for human and environmental health, and the lowest in-use cost option, in fact, lowest in-use cost.

Here the Sustainability Scorecard was helpful in identifying methodologies to optimize the solution and even the operations. The Coastwide product team led by Roger took bold steps to completely eliminate all toxic chemicals from their products. This product innovation required drop-in replacements with sustainable chemical alternatives that improved the efficiency and overall performance of the line. Further, to address waste prevention from a transportation standpoint, the team even redesigned product containers to an S shape and optimized the bottle thickness to ensure durability of the container and to reduce the breakage of bottles during transport. Once the number of bottles in each container had been optimized, the team went even further to create circularity in transportation materials. Wooden pallets are typically used during lifting and moving activities. However, once the products have been transported on top of pallets, these material components end up as waste, and typically find their way into a landfill as a graveyard. Roger McFadden's team created an additional revenue stream out of resale of pallets once their use was completed.

Set your suppliers up for success. Coastwide worked with its suppliers in marketing the suppliers own formulations to other customers. This built a coalition of firms with green procurement strategies, enabling greater sales in the "green" space for suppliers.

Get everyone on board. With Coastwide radically reassessing and redesigning its processes, the process of training every stakeholder in sales and among external suppliers began. The company created three levels of education to convey its value proposition to its different audiences: employees, suppliers, and customers.

Employees. As Roger McFadden told us, when you educate your own organization well first, everything works better externally. Ineffective chemical management can affect product performance and environment quality, the negative effects of which affect business reputation and brand integrity. The company made sure the sales professionals knew why each chemical reformulation had occurred and empowered them to educate their peers and customers.

Suppliers. Coastwide collaborated with well-informed and engaged leaders at suppliers to potentially source even more effective ingredients for the organization. Coastwide used this opportunity to educate its suppliers on green chemistry and the company's goals related to continuous improvement. The company informed them of the economic factors that determined inputs, and once suppliers began recognizing that Coastwide's advances in green chemistry formulation would be marketable to their other customers, they were on board.

Coastwide met with supplier Rohm & Haas in 2002 to discuss concerns over zinc and other metals used to bind with acrylics in floor polishes. Following the meeting, Rohm & Haas designed and introduced the first zinc-free polymer emulsion in the industry, which Coastwide then used in its Sustainable Earth floor polish. Coastwide pursued similar positive changes with suppliers Akzo Nobel and Novozyme. When one supplier failed to commit to Coastwide's new objectives, Coastwide switched to a new partner who was able to provide a superior, safer chemical ingredient to meet the Coastwide criteria

Customers. Coastwide utilized an extensive customer feedback and education policy. Its sales department invested in educating customers about the benefits of using the new formulations and the ancillary costs that were negated in the process—for example, costs related to the need for personal protective equipment such as gloves and masks, and to corrosion on hard material surfaces. Also, Roger explains, they were encouraged to go as far as breaking down the costs for the customer. These clear benefits of the sustainable product lines informed the firm's "lowest-total-cost provider" status for its clients. And to the firm's surprise, customers not only loved the sustainable products, but they were willing to pay 10 percent more than the traditional products.

The success of the Sustainable Earth line led to an enterprise-wide focus on green cleaning products for Coastwide. And once Corporate Express/Staples sniffed out the firm's alignment with its own corporate mission to offer its customers safer products, the company eventually acquired Coastwide.

Coastwide's success (and attractiveness to Staples) can be attributed to the circular nature of its processes. The company closed the loop on everything, including its supply chain.

At the time, Coastwide had amassed more than ten thousand industrial and commercial customers, with an suprisingly low customer turnover of less than 2 percent a year. By converting to sustainability in its service lines, the firm risked long-term relationships with customers who were accustomed to the effectiveness and efficiency of existing products at existing price points. In addition, the firm faced stiff competition in the cleaning goods marketplace.

So Coastwide brought one distribution function and two manufacturing units under its own label. This improved its negotiating power with suppliers so that its price points could remain competitive. Now, not only did it manufacture a full line of commercial cleaning chemicals such as cleaners, disinfectants, floor finishes, and degreasers but it was also a full-line distributor of sanitary maintenance supplies to companies such as 3M, Advance, Georgia-Pacific, Heritage, Johnson Wax, Rubbermaid, and Windsor. Of the $13.6 million in chemical sales during 2004, Coastwide's private-label chemical sales accounted for nearly half, $6 million, a $600,000 increase over the previous year.

CHALLENGES TO SCALING SUSTAINABILITY

Scaling a green organization doesn't happen in a bubble. It requires innovation, collaboration, and incentives. Here are some of the initiatives Staples/Coastwide and other market shapers have implemented and what you can learn from their success.

1. **Innovating the supplier strategy.** As the Staples/ Coastwide case study shows, educating suppliers is one of the most effective levers in supply-chain redesign. Coastwide's race to the top strategy focused on supplier collaboration and competition beyond price. The company asked its suppliers to find innovative solutions for the packaging, manufacturing, and distribution challenges it faced with its sustainable products.

For market shapers that are looking to further refine their supplier strategy, we recommend leveraging the Sustainability Scorecard. By asking suppliers to provide inputs that align with the scorecard metrics, firms can force and customize innovation in their procurement. For large firms such as Staples that buy sustainable firms like Coastwide to scale their sustainability offerings, demanding better sustainability metrics from their suppliers can reduce barriers related to supplier strategy. In particular, the scorecard's principle of waste prevention can further firms' goals to build more transparency in their supply chains. When firms such as Staples and other large players demand reporting along forward-facing metrics and supply chain transformations, they can go a long way in nudging suppliers to increase their due diligence.

Due to the fragmented and complex nature of today's supply chains, along with the patented or proprietary formulations sourced by suppliers, firms can often fail to disclose complete ingredient lists. Further, supply chains today tend to be tiered, wherein tier 1 represents the direct supplier from which the retailer has procured the ingredient, and tier 2 represents the supplier to the tier 1 supplier, and so on. This complexity can create disclosure gaps, but firms can at minimum require suppliers to disclose the inputs that they consider "bad actors" and that they have committed to not providing to their customers. Ensuring that these bad actors are eliminated from supply chains can help increase transparency, while maintaining compliance with proprietary formulations.

2. **Collaborating with strange bedfellows.** Market shapers can consider partnering with third-party organizations and other groups to create industry-wide sustainability standards and certifications using the Sustainability Scorecard.

Another important type of collaboration is with research organizations and even competitors to problem-solve together and create circularity. Philips leverages partnerships to codevelop solutions with universities, healthcare systems, and analytics firms to create relationships that are focused on evolving problem statements, rather than business models that focus on one-time transactions and solutions.

Last, coalitions and partnerships with nonprofits and associations with industry data in certain regions may be able to provide you directional, albeit imperfect data regarding opaque supply chains. It is not perfect and, yes, it is a challenge to address opacity, but it is important to take the first step in creating visibility into the origin of inputs. Taking such actions and developing coalitions can often lead to first-mover advantages by way of differentiated supply chains that are "cleaner" and can be verified, to a degree. This increases consumer confidence in the firm over time—and consumers are watching.

3. **Funding a promising solution.** Investing in the organizations innovating in your industry can help accelerate progress from the lab to the marketplace. For example, P2 Science, an innovative chemistry company, develops entirely new chemicals that can serve as foundational platforms on which cosmetics and fragrance firms can build clean and sustainable makeup formulations. These formulations, which start from an entirely sustainable base of renewable inputs and benign chemicals, create radical opportunities for large firms that seek to capture additional market share and address consumer demand for safe beauty products.

Sustainable Earth's®
Sustainability Score

The Sustainable Earth line was a pioneer among cleaning products and was the first to be recognized by the EPA for its green chemistry formulations. These benign-by-design products were the result of innovation and targeted redefinition, reengineering, and optimization. For fun, we decided to score the Sustainable Earth line in order to provide a more in-depth view of how the Sustainability Scorecard works.

Please note: The scoring here was performed by the authors in a retrospective manner after reviewing publicly available literature on the Sustainable Earth line. Although we have provided a more comprehensive scorecard later in this book, here we will highlight some of the key metrics on which Sustainable Earth moved the needle:

1. Waste prevention
   a. Process mass intensity (PMI): Conservation of water and energy and other key chemicals in the new formulations. More than 50% less water needed.
   b. Environmental quotient index (EQI): The elimination of environmentally and human-health-related toxic chemicals such as phthalates (endocrine-disrupting chemicals) and other known carcinogens resulted in a favorable "environmental friendliness" quotient for this service line.
2. Maximizing efficiency and performance: the Sustainable Earth line was highly favorable in performance due to the following:
   a. Cost efficiency: Lower total cost to its customers (enabled through the concentrated cleaning product innovation) and positive impacts on the firm's gross margins up to 40% higher than traditional cleaning products.
   b. Effectiveness: The products were 63% more effective in stain removal.
3. Renewable inputs that remove fossil fuels entirely from the formulation development process
4. Safe degradation
   a. Time/exposure: The green chemistry used to develop these products resulted in benign chemicals on degradation, resulting in low bioaccumulation, no persistence, and low exposure.

Every business leader understands the need to seize opportunities and capture value. Gundersen Health Systems' $2 million investment into energy efficiency has paid off with a $1.2 million annual reduction in energy costs for the hospital system. Coastwide's (now Staples') Sustainable Earth service-line transformation has successfully created significant value propositions for its janitorial client base in terms of regulatory and market-leading differentiation. As both Gundersen and Staples show, designing a future that is healthful, replenishing, circular, and effective in leveraging climate economics can be your greatest unexpected business opportunity.

Conclusion

If It's Not Profitable, It's Not Sustainable

To continue to accept these realities is *absurdity*.

To not do anything about them is *obscenity*.

To not profit from the unexpected solutions that sustainability offers would be *humankind's greatest missed opportunity*.

—*Paul Anastas*

For the better part of a decade, firms have led the charge with sustainability initiatives designed to address the climate crisis. Efforts have largely centered around supply chains and sourcing, reduction of carbon emissions, recycling, and support of local communities—all spokes on the wheel that supports the well-being of the planet and its inhabitants. But can these efforts really survive if they remain separate from a focus on profitability?

One of the reasons why climate change and sustainability get so much attention these days is that the economic shock to businesses has become so high. So high that even the Big Four accounting firms are finally auditing ESG (environmental, social, governmental) metrics.

Our hope in writing this book and offering the Sustainability Scorecard is that more firms will begin recognizing that environmental and financial sustainability go hand in hand, that by leveraging our framework they can stay ahead of industry trends with unexpected solutions that create long-term business value.

In the short term, it won't be easy, we know. The actions firms and leaders take today to integrate meaningful and sustainable innovation into their systems will require them not only to challenge their perceptions but also to invest intellectually and financially in redesigning current systems. Furthermore, sustainable solutions don't yet exist for all the products and processes that drive our current economy. Oh, and the status quo will lie through its teeth to preserve itself.

There are several scorecards out there that approach climate-change economics and business decision-making from an investment standpoint, a value realization perspective, or a risk management perspective; however, none of them are driven by science. Each of the chemistry and engineering principles that we have leveraged to create the Sustainability Scorecard has been peer-reviewed scientifically, giving it a degree of credibility that no other scorecard has. You can be assured that progress on the Sustainability Scorecard metrics is really moving your firm toward greater sustainability. Our hope is that seeing how the actions you take actually move its metrics—while providing innovative new solutions—will give you and your firm the determination to stay the course. And to scale.

The Role of Unexpected Solutions in Achieving the UN Sustainable Development Goals

In 2015, the United Nations unveiled the seventeen Sustainable Development Goals (SDGs) in order to provide global audiences with an overarching framework toward which efforts could be aligned. We believe that the most impactful role in accelerating progress toward the SDGs lies in systematic scaling of unexpected solutions.

Unexpected solutions, as we have discussed earlier in this book, are unique for several reasons:

- Unexpected solutions are leapfrog solutions. They have, in many respects, maximized the F-factor—the qualitative metric that we discuss in the scorecard. F-factor is a forward-looking metric to better understand the value proposition of any new product or process, in which to maximize function, the weight of the inputs has to be minimized. What this forecasts for product and process of the future is to provide directionality to our innovation efforts. Specifically, the F-factor indicates that innovation should occur in such a manner that we achieve all the benefits of the product or process *without the inputs ever existing*. In the case of communication services, this led to smartphones—wherein all the functionality of the telephone is present without the presence of telephone wires and other infrastructural elements.

    The life-cycle benefits of such as solutions are also optimized, as these solutions typically have minimized costs over the entire life cycle of the solution.

- These solutions are inherently sustainable and fulfill the Twelve Principles of Green Chemistry. For example, unexpected solutions rely on renewable resources, a lever in favor of a bio-based economy. Although chemical production only accounts for 5%–7% of petroleum consumption, petroleum sources represent over 98% of chemical feedstocks. Unexpected solutions find alternative routes to powering performance.

- They are usually able to achieve multiple goals simultaneously, in comparison to traditional solutions that align with only one major and/or a few minor problem statements. In such a scenario, big-picture thinking—such as the SDGs—can clearly articulate the various parameters along which the value is provided.

- Unexpected solutions further equity by solving particularly wicked problems for various industries. For example, inherently safe chemical sites prevent accidents that would ultimately affect entire geographies. Reducing the social and environmental impacts of "forever chemicals" (or eliminating them altogether) from manufacturing of everyday products has the potential to significantly reduce the total cost of care for large population subsets in healthcare and to improve the public health outcomes for vulnerable communities, all while improving financial outcomes for organizations.

These unexpected solutions are operational game changers and enable firms to realize financial benefits—in the form of reduced operational expenses, additional revenue streams, additional market share, increased profitability, or even all of the above. This coupled with social and environmental profitability expands firm performance along the new definition of performance. These outcomes not only exponentially increase the overall profitability of firms but usher firms into new economic territory that aligns their outcomes with the SDGs.

Sustainability does not belong in risk management, and it's not a niche marketing advantage, although that's the way many boards and leaders see it today. It is a business imperative, a strategy and operations input with compelling financial benefits. But we should not sit back and accept this reality. We need to move beyond risk management in order to create real, transformational, revenue-generating opportunities from sustainability, rather than just playing whack-a-mole with audit reports. We need to design our products and processes to be sustainable—and we need to profit from doing so. Anything less will be humankind's greatest missed opportunity.

Example Scorecards

I n the next sections, we have provided examples of completed scorecards from the case studies described previously in this book.

Coastwide Labs/Staples

As described within this book, Coastwide Laboratories (later acquired
by Staples) created a sustainability transformation within its organization. The scorecard here was leveraged by Coastwide to understand
the operational sustainability of their successful Sustainable Earth line
of products. This evaluation is an assessment of the chemical formulation of the Sustainable Earth line as well as the business operations of
the same service line.

SCORECARD COMPONENT
PART 1: WASTE PREVENTION

KPI	SUB-METRIC	TRADITIONAL PRODUCT: BEFORE SUSTAINABILITY TRANSFORMATION	UNEXPECTED SOLUTION: SUSTAINABLE EARTH®	RATING
Economy of waste	Atom economy (in g/mol, percentage)	50%	90%–100%	0
	E-factor	Over 50	1–4	0
	Packaging: percentage of readily recyclable material	10%–20%	100%	0
Economy of space	Number of units per square foot of product	25% wasted space in packaging	0% wasted space S-shaped bottles allowed for no space to be wasted	0
	Number of units transported per vehicle	25	48	0
Process intensification	Productivity/size ratio Productivity/weight ratio	0	100%	0

Part 1 qualitative analysis: Prior to the sustainability transformation of Sustainable Earth, the service line demonstrated waste in two main areas:

- The chemical formulation itself
- Packaging and transportation

The firm took steps to alter the chemical formulation along the lines of the green chemistry that specifically improved the atom economy, E-factor, and process intensification (waste metrics of chemical formulations) so as to reduce waste and create savings related to operational expenses.

Within packaging, the firm altered the shape of the bottles that were used to transport the cleaning material. The new S-shaped bottles with optimized bottle thickness not only enabled 25 percent more product to fit within a shipping container but also reduced the breakage rate of bottles during transport. This in and of itself optimized the number of total units transported per vehicle, bringing the eventual number of boxes transported up to forty-eight (from an original twenty-five). This increased operational savings further by reducing the number of trips and fuel consumption in transporting the product to suppliers.

SCORECARD COMPONENT
PART 2: MAXIMIZING EFFICIENCY AND PERFORMANCE

KPI	SUB-METRIC	TRADITIONAL PRODUCT: BEFORE SUSTAINABILITY TRANSFORMATION	UNEXPECTED SOLUTION: SUSTAINABLE EARTH ®	RATING
Material efficiency	Mass of recycled material/total mass Mass of renewable material/total mass	40%	90%–100%	0
Environmental health metrics	Global warming potential (in kg CO_2 emissions)	298	Negligible	1
	Acidification potential (in kg CO_2 equivalents)	High	Negligible	1
	Eutrophication potential (in kg N equivalents)	High	Negligible	1
	Ozone depletion potential (in kg CDC 11 equivalents)	High	Negligible	1

PART 2: MAXIMIZING EFFICIENCY AND PERFORMANCE (continued)

KPI	SUB-METRIC	TRADITIONAL PRODUCT: BEFORE SUSTAINABILITY TRANSFORMATION	UNEXPECTED SOLUTION: SUSTAINABLE EARTH ®	RATING
	Smog formation potential (kg O emissions)	High	Negligible	1
Human health metrics	Number of restricted chemicals according to EU and US guidelines	90%	0	0
	Percentage of chemicals linked to high acuity, disease, and procedural complexity (i.e., high-cost patients)	70%	0	0
	Percentage of chemicals linked to high acuity, disease, and procedural complexity (i.e., moder-ately high-cost patients)	10%	0	0

(continued)

PART 2: MAXIMIZING EFFICIENCY AND PERFORMANCE (continued)

KPI	SUB-METRIC	TRADITIONAL PRODUCT: BEFORE SUSTAINABILITY TRANSFORMATION	UNEXPECTED SOLUTION: SUSTAINABLE EARTH ®	RATING
	Percentage of chemicals with robust data sources on assessment of health impacts	30%	100%	0

Part 2 discussion: Coastwide created a positive environmental and human health impact by eliminating 100 percent of toxic chemicals that were associated with cancer or designed to persist in the human body throughout generations (demonstrating transgenerational design, as we described earlier in this book). Toxic chemical compounds such as FAE blends, APG, AO, 9.5 EO, ethylene glycol monobutyl ether, branched alkyl benzene sulfonates, and endocrine-disrupting chemicals were all eliminated and replaced with environmentally and biologically benign formulations. Further, this new methodology required 50 percent less water for rinsing after use of the cleaning products.[1]

As reported by Darden Business Publishing at University of Virginia, these sustainability transformations that "assumed lower risk through use of benign products would ultimately translate into lower insurance premiums, lower handling costs, fewer sick days, less expense for protective equipment, lower regulatory burdens and expenses, elimination of hazardous material handling training, and lower waste disposal costs. TriMet and a few school districts had already reported a reduction in the number of sick days ascribed to chemical-related injuries or sickness." Further, Darden reported that "the Sustainable Earth line enabled Coastwide to lower its customers' costs for maintenance by offering system solutions. Higher dilution rates for chemicals, dispensing units that eliminated overuse, improved safety for the end user, and less lost work time because of health problems associated with chemical exposure were reported.

TriMet, the Portland, Oregon, metropolitan area's municipal bus and light rail system, reduced its number of cleaning products from twenty-two to four by switching to Sustainable Earth. Initial cleaning-chemical cost savings to the municipality amounted to 70 percent, not including training cost savings associated with the inventory simplification. In 2006, the Sustainable Earth line performed as well as or better than the market category leaders while realizing a gross margin more than 40 percent higher than on the company's conventional cleaners."[2]

SCORECARD COMPONENT
PART 3: RENEWABLE INPUTS

KPI	SUB-METRIC	TRADITIONAL PRODUCT	UNEXPECTED SOLUTION: SUSTAINABLE EARTH®	RATING
Renewable carbon-free energy inputs	Percentage renewable carbon			
Percentage of carbon-negative carbon	20%	95%–100%	0	

(continued)

PART 3: RENEWABLE INPUTS (continued)

KPI	SUB-METRIC	TRADITIONAL PRODUCT	UNEXPECTED SOLUTION: SUSTAINABLE EARTH®	RATING
Waste energy utilization		20%	80%	0
Renewable feedstocks	Percentage of total inputs that are derived from renewable resources	20%	80%	0

Part 3 discussion: The new chemical formulations were readily biodegradable and had nearly zero volatile compounds. Volatile compounds are substances that evaporate at room temperature and in many cases persist in the environment and even act as biomarkers for certain cancers. The sustainability transformation brought these chemicals down to zero and thereby reduced exposure as well.

SCORECARD COMPONENT
PART 4: SAFE DEGRADATION

KPI	SUB-METRIC	TRADITIONAL PRODUCT: BEFORE SUSTAINABILITY TRANSFORMATION	UNEXPECTED SOLUTION: SUSTAINABLE EARTH®	RATING
Persistence (a measure of trans-generational design)	Percentage of "forever chemicals" in final product	70%	0	0
Bioaccumulation	Bioaccumulation factor	High	0	0

Part 4 discussion: The firm scaled the input of renewable resources for the production of chemical formulations as well as the use of waste energy to capture otherwise lost energy The only area where renewable energy was not leveraged was in the trucks that transported the goods to suppliers.

P2Science

This assessment was conducted by P2Science in Nagatuck, Connecticut, to compare its product Citropol® H to a traditional input to cosmetics and hair products: silicones (specifically, dimethicones). Silicones are chemically inert components of cosmetics that function to smooth hair and skin, giving foundation and other makeup a smoother, almost air-brushed distribution. They can even help control the thickness of the product that is applied to skin, which helps hold the moisture in the skin and prevent dryness.

SCORECARD COMPONENT
PART 1: WASTE PREVENTION

KPI	SUB-METRIC	TRADITIONAL PRODUCT: SILICONE (DIMETHICONE)	UNEXPECTED SOLUTION: CITROPOL® H	RATING
Economy of waste	Atom economy (in g/mol, percentage)	Less than 50%	>95%	0
	E-factor	Over 50	<1	0
	Reaction yield	Less than 50%	>95%	0
Economy of space	One-pot synthesis	No	Yes	0
Process intensification	Productivity/size ratio	Not continuous, and process is not intensified	100% continous and process intensified	0

Part 1 qualitative analysis: Traditional silicones (brand agnostic) are typically highly wasteful in the design phase, resulting in low yield in comparison to the waste produced in the chemical reaction. P2Science's process resulted in over 95 percent yield (i.e., there was minimal chemical waste), and the company even conducted the reaction in one pot to prevent the use of a large volume of reactors and equipment. This metric can have a significant effect on the PP&E (property, plant, and equipment) line item in financial reports.

SCORECARD COMPONENT
PART 2: MAXIMIZING EFFICIENCY AND PERFORMANCE

KPI	SUB-METRIC	TRADITIONAL PRODUCT: SILICONE (DIMETHICONE)	UNEXPECTED SOLUTION: CITROPOL® H	RATING
Material efficiency	Mass of recycled material/total mass Mass of renewable material/total mass	High	100%	0
Environmental health metrics	Global warming potential (in $kg\ CO_2$ emissions)	High	Negligible	0
	Acidification potential (in $kg\ CO_2$ emissions)	High	Negligible	0
	Eutrophication potential (in kg N emissions)	High	Negligible	0
	Ozone depletion potential (in kg CDC 11 emissions)	High	Negligible	0

(continued)

PART 2: MAXIMIZING EFFICIENCY AND PERFORMANCE (continued)

KPI	SUB-METRIC	TRADITIONAL PRODUCT: SILICONE (DIMETHICONE)	UNEXPECTED SOLUTION: CITROPOL® H	RATING
	Smog formation potential (kg O emissions)	High	Negligible	0
Human health metrics	Number of restricted chemicals according to EU and US guidelines	80%	0	0
	Percentage of chemicals linked to high acuity, disease, and procedural complexity (i.e. high-cost patients)	60%	0	0
	Percentage of chemicals linked to high acuity, disease, and procedural complexity (i.e. moderately high-cost patients)	40%	0	0

PART 2: MAXIMIZING EFFICIENCY AND PERFORMANCE (continued)

KPI	SUB-METRIC	TRADITIONAL PRODUCT: SILICONE (DIMETHICONE)	UNEXPECTED SOLUTION: CITROPOL® H	RATING
	Percentage of chemicals with robust data sources on assessment of health impacts	40%	100	0

Part 2 qualitative analysis: Most silicones not only degrade as microplastics in the environment but also result in reproductive and other toxicology-related negative externalities. Citropol® H is entirely benign as it relates to toxicology and other high-, moderate-, and even low-risk health effects.

SCORECARD COMPONENT
PART 3: RENEWABLE RESOURCES

KPI	SUB-METRIC	TRADITIONAL PRODUCT: SILICONE (DIMETHICONE)	UNEXPECTED SOLUTION: CITROPOL® H	RATING
Renewable carbon-free energy inputs	Percentage of renewable carbon / Percentage of carbon-negative carbon	0–10%	100% renewable electricity	0
Waste energy utilization		0–10%	0%	0
Renewable feedstocks	Percentage of total inputs that are derived from renewable resources	0%	100%	0

Part 3 qualitative analysis: All supply chain inputs and the entire production of Citropol® H leverage over 95 percent of renewable inputs.

SCORECARD COMPONENT
PART 4: SAFE DEGRADATION

KPI	SUB-METRIC	TRADITIONAL PRODUCT: SILICONE (DIMETHICONE)	UNEXPECTED SOLUTION: CITROPOL® H	RATING
Persistence (a measure of transgenerational design)	Percentage of "forever chemicals" in final product	100%	0	0
Bioaccumulation	Bioaccumulation factor	High	0	0
Exposure	Induction period and duration of product life	High	0	0
	Latent period and duration of product life	High	0	0

Koninklijke Philips N.V.

This assessment was provided by Philips N.V. to demonstrate the environmental and health-related effectiveness of their upcycling and refurbished medical devices service line.

SCORECARD COMPONENT
PART 1: WASTE PREVENTION

KPI	SUB-METRIC	TRADITIONAL PRODUCT	UNEXPECTED SOLUTION: REFURBISHED MEDICAL DEVICES AND EQUIPMENT	RATING
Economy of waste	Percentage of mass of upcycled material/total mass of product	50%	90%–100%	0
	Packaging: percentage of readily recyclable material	10%–20%	100% in OR	0
	Extended product life (in years)	0	+ 20 years (approximately) in the case of MRI machines and other durable medical equipment	0

Part 1 qualitative analysis: Prior to the sustainability transformation, Philips had no visibility into its supply chain after the medical devices were collected by end users. By way of introducing a collection-and-refurbishment methodology, the firm created operational expense savings, extended the product life, and were able to leverage revenue through an increased number of sales per product.

SCORECARD COMPONENT
PART 2: MAXIMIZING EFFICIENCY
AND PERFORMANCE

KPI	SUB-METRIC	TRADITIONAL PRODUCT	UNEXPECTED SOLUTION: REFURBISHED MEDICAL DEVICES AND EQUIPMENT	RATING
Material efficiency	Mass of recycled material/total mass Mass of renewable material/total mass	0%	90%–100%	0
Environmental health metrics	Global warming potential (in kg CO_2 emissions)	Net increase in GWP due to increased material and energy use in production	Neutralized	1
	Acidification potential (in kg CO_2 emissions)	Net increase in AP due to increased material and energy use in production	Neutralized	1
	Eutrophication potential (in kg N emissions)	Net increase in EP	Neutralized	1
	Ozone depletion potential (in kg CDC 11 emissions)	Net increase in ODP	Neutralized	1

(continued)

PART 2: MAXIMIZING EFFICIENCY AND PERFORMANCE (continued)

KPI	SUB-METRIC	TRADITIONAL PRODUCT	UNEXPECTED SOLUTION: REFURBISHED MEDICAL DEVICES AND EQUIPMENT	RATING
	Smog formation potential (kg O emissions)	Increase in SFP	Neutralized	1
Human health metrics	Number of restricted chemicals according to EU and US guidelines	0%	0	2
	Percentage of chemicals linked to high acuity, disease, and procedural complexity (i.e., high-cost patients)	50%	Low, 0–10%	2
	Percentage of chemicals linked to high acuity, disease and procedural complexity (i.e., moderately high-cost patients)	50%	0–10%	2

PART 2: MAXIMIZING EFFICIENCY AND
PERFORMANCE (continued)

KPI	SUB-METRIC	TRADITIONAL PRODUCT	UNEXPECTED SOLUTION: REFURBISHED MEDICAL DEVICES AND EQUIPMENT	RATING
	Percentage of chemicals with robust data sources on assessment of health impacts	10%	0–10%	2

Part 2 qualitative analysis: Reclaiming chemicals and components that would otherwise pose negative health effects in landfills or other modes of end of life, the firm was able to upcycle these components in an environmentally benign manner. This eliminates the health effects to humans by way of groundwater contamination and the like, and keeps unsustainable products in circulation in the economy, ultimately avoiding a graveyard end of life.

SCORECARD COMPONENT
PART 3: RENEWABLE RESOURCES

KPI	SUB-METRIC	TRADITIONAL PRODUCT	UNEXPECTED SOLUTION: REFURBISHED MEDICAL DEVICES AND EQUIPMENT	RATING
Renewable carbon-free energy inputs	Percentage of renewable carbon Percentage of carbon-negative carbon	0%	75% carbon neutral	0
Waste energy utilization		0%	75%	0
Renewable feedstocks	Percentage of total inputs that are derived from renewable resources	0%	75%	0

Part 3 qualitative analysis: Philips currently leverages 75 percent renewable energy and is on track to attain 100 percent renewable energy for all business practices.

SCORECARD COMPONENT
PART 4: SAFE DEGRADATION

KPI	SUB-METRIC	TRADITIONAL PRODUCT	UNEXPECTED SOLUTION: REFURBISHED MEDICAL DEVICES AND EQUIPMENT	RATING
Persistence (a measure of transgenerational design)	Percentage of "forever chemicals" in final product	60%	0	1
Bioaccumulation	Bioaccumulation factor	High	0	1
Exposure	Induction period and duration of product life	High	0	1
	Latent period and duration of product life	High	0	1

Notes

Introduction

1. University of Michigan, "Fuel Efficiency of Vehicles on the Road: Little Progress since the 1920s," May 5, 2009, https://news.umich.edu/fuel -efficiency-of-vehicles-on-the-road-little-progress-since-the-1920s/.
2. Richard Snow, *I Invented the Modern Age: The Rise of Henry Ford* (Thorndike, ME: Simon & Schuster, 2014).
3. Henry Ford and Samuel Crowther, *My Life and Work* (Garden City, NY: Doubleday, Page & Co., 1922).
4. A&E Television Networks, "Ford Motor Company Unveils the Model T," edited by History.com editors, November 13, 2009, https://www.history .com/this-day-in-history/ford-motor-company-unveils-the-model-t.
5. Ford and Crowther. *My Life and Work.*
6. Ford and Crowther.
7. Snow, *I Invented the Modern Age.*
8. Snow.
9. Angela Rawlings, "Why Iceland Held a Glacier Funeral," *Reykjavík Grapevine*, August 30, 2019, https://grapevine.is/news/2019/08/30/why -iceland-held-a-glacier-funeral/.
10. Government of Iceland, Ministry for the Environment and Natural Resources, "Climate Change," June 28, 2021, https://www.government.is /topics/environment-climate-and-nature-protection/climate-change/.
11. Environment Agency of Iceland, *National Inventory Report, Iceland 2020*, United Nations Framework on Climate Change, 2020, https://unfccc.int /documents/225487.
12. Paul Hawken, *Natural Capitalism: Creating the Next Industrial Revolution* (Boston: Little, Brown, 1999).

13. Hawken, *Natural Capitalism*.
14. Hawken.
15. Matthew J. Eckelman and Jodi D. Sherman, "Estimated Global Disease Burden From US Health Care Sector Greenhouse Gas Emissions," *American Journal of Public Health* 108, Suppl 2 (2108): S120–22. doi: 10.2105/AJPH.2017.303846.
16. Center for Sustainable Systems, University of Michigan, "U.S. Environmental Footprint Factsheet," September 1, 2020, http://css.umich.edu/factsheets/us-environmental-footprint-factsheet.
17. Bill Gates, "No Masks or Capes, but These Heroes Are Saving the World," Gates Notes, September 1, 2020, https://www.gatesnotes.com/About-Bill-Gates/These-Heroes-Are-Saving-the-World.
18. Zied Guedri and Xavier Hollandts, "Beyond Dichotomy: The Curvilinear Impact of Employee Ownership on Firm Performance," *Corporate Governance: An International Review*, 16, no. 5 (2008): 460–74.

Chapter 1

1. Patrick Alan Kent, *A History of the Pyrrhic War* (Abingdon, United Kingdom: Routledge, 2020).
2. Kent, *History*.
3. Dana Nuccitell, "Climate Change Could Cost U.S. Economy Billions," *Yale Climate Connections*, April 29, 2019, https://yaleclimateconnections.org/2019/04/climate-change-could-cost-u-s-economy-billions/.
4. Nuccitell, "Climate Change."
5. Nuccitell.
6. Plastics Industry Association, *Size & Impact Report* (Washington, DC: Plastics Industry Association, 2020).
7. Plastics Industry Association, *Size & Impact Report*.
8. Ottmar Edenhofer, Ramón Pichs Madruga, Youba Sokona, Susanne Kadner, Jan Cristoph Minx, Steffen Brunner, et al., *Technical Summary: Climate Change 2014: Mitigation of Climate Change. Contribution of Working Group III to the Fifth Assessment Report of the Intergovernmental Panel on Climate Change* (Cambridge, United Kingdom: Cambridge University Press, 2014).
9. Edenhofer et al., *Technical Summary*.
10. Thomas Czigler, Sebastian Reiter, Patrick Schulze, and Ken Somers, "Laying the Foundation for Zero-Carbon Cement," McKinsey & Company, May 14, 2020, https://www.mckinsey.com/industries/chemicals/our-insights/laying-the-foundation-for-zero-carbon-cement.

11. Czigler et al., "Laying the Foundation."

12. *PBS NewsHour*, "This Cement Alternative Absorbs CO2 Like a Sponge," pbs.org, April 13, 2015, https://www.pbs.org/newshour/show/cement-alternative-absorbs-carbon-dioxide-like-sponge.

13. Alejandro Lanuza Garcia, Ashik Thithira Achaiah, John Bello, and Thomas Donovan, *Ferrock: A Life Cycle Comparison to Ordinary Portland Cement*, University of Southern California, 2017.

14. "Build Abroad, Ferrock: A Stronger, Greener Alternative to Concrete?" Build Abroad, Accessed October 1, 2021, https://www.buildabroad.org/2016/09/27/Ferrock/.

15. Environmental Protection Agency, "Tribal ecoAmbassadors 2011–2012 Program," 2011, https://archive.epa.gov/ecoambassadors/web/pdf/2011-2012-tribal-ecoambassadors-report.pdf.

16. EPA, "Tribal ecoAmbassadors."

17. EPA.

18. Czigler et al., "Laying the Foundation."

19. Milton Friedman and Rose D. Friedman, *Capitalism and Freedom* (Chicago: University of Chicago Press, 1962).

20. Christine Bader and Wesley Longhofer, "Opinion: This Long-Standing Tenet of American Capitalism Must Change—Now," Institute on the Environment, University of Minnesota, September 24, 2020, https://ensia.com/voices/business-captialism-social-responsibility-profit-milton-friedman-environment-economic-inequality/.

Chapter 2

1. Ellen MacArthur Foundation, *A New Textiles Economy*, January 12, 2017, https://emf.thirdlight.com/link/2axvc7eob8zx-za4ule/@/preview/1?o.

2. Julie Beth Zimmerman, "Minimizing Unintended Consequences," Walter J. Weber, Jr. Distinguished Lecture in Environmental and Energy Sustainability, 2014. Available on YouTube, https://www.youtube.com/watch?v=dzH5JEYH9-k.

3. Zimmerman, "Minimizing."

4. Zimmerman.

5. Union of Concerned Scientists, *Environmental Impacts of Solar Power* (Washington, DC: Union of Concerned Scientists, 2013).

6. Union of Concerned Scientists, *Environmental Impacts*.

7. US Environmental Protection Agency, "Information about the Green Chemistry Challenge," last updated October 13, 2021, https://www.epa.gov/greenchemistry/information-about-green-chemistry-challenge.

8. Jeff Sonnenfeld and Daniel Esty, "An Earth Day CEO Summit Shows How Dramatically Corporate Values Have Changed," *Fortune*, April 22, 2020, https://fortune.com/2020/04/22/earth-day-sustainability-ceo-summit/.

9. U.S. Chemical Safety and Hazard Investigation Board. "Key Lessons for Preventing Inadvertent Mixing During Chemical Unloading Operations," October 21, 2016, https://www.csb.gov/assets/1/20/mgpi_case_study.pdf?15915.

Chapter 3

1. Martin J. Mulvihill, Evan S. Beach, Julie B. Zimmerman, and Paul T. Anastas, "Green Chemistry and Green Engineering: A Framework for Sustainable Technology Development," *Annual Review of Environment and Resources* 26 (2011): 271–93, https://doi.org/10.1146/annurev-environ-032009-095500.

2. Edward R. Monteith, Pieter Mampuys, Louise Summerton, James H. Clark, Bert U.W. Maes, and Con Robert McElroy, "Why We Might Be Misusing Process Mass Intensity (PMI) and a Methodology to Apply It Effectively as a Discovery Level Metric," *Green Chemistry* 21, no. 1 (2019): 123–35.

3. Cornell University College of Agricultural and Life Sciences, Cornell Turfgrass Program, "Environmental Impact Quotient (EIQ) Explained," n.d., https://turf.cals.cornell.edu/pests-and-weeds/environmental-impact-quotient-eiq-explained/.

4. US House of Representatives Committee on Science and Technology, "Hearing on: 'E-Waste R&D Act,'" testimony of Paul T. Anastas and Julie B. Zimmerman, February 9, 2009, https://republicans-science.house.gov/sites/republicans.science.house.gov/files/documents/hearings/021109Anastas.pdf.

5. US House of Representatives, "Hearing."

6. US House of Representatives.

7. Environmental Protection Agency, "National Overview: Facts and Figures on Materials, Wastes and Recycling," last updated July 14, 2021, https://www.epa.gov/facts-and-figures-about-materials-waste-and-recycling/national-overview-facts-and-figures-materials.

8. Paul T. Anastas and Julie B. Zimmerman, "Design through the 12 Principles of Green Engineering," *Environmental Science & Technology* 37, no. 5 (2003): 94A–101A, https://doi.org/10.1021/es032373g.

9. Concepcion Jimenez-Gonzalez, Celia S. Ponder, Quirinus B. Broxterman, and Julie B. Manley, "Using the Right Green Yardstick: Why Process Mass Intensity Is Used in the Pharmaceutical Industry to Drive More Sustainable Processes," *Organic Process Research & Development* 15, no. 4 (May 12, 2011): 912–17. https://doi.org/10.1021/op200097d.

10. Jimenez-Gonzalez et al., "Using the Right Green Yardstick."

11. Kristi Budzinski, Megan Blewis, Philip Dahlin, Daniel D'Aquila, Julia Esparza, Jack Gavin, Sa V. Ho, Clarice Hutchens, et al., "Introduction of a Process Mass Intensity Metric for Biologics," *New Biotechnology* 49 (March 25, 2019): 37–42, http://dx.doi.org/10.1016/j.nbt.2018.07.005.

12. Lisa Jarvis, "Life after Zocor," *Chemical & Engineering News*, August 24, 2006, https://cen.acs.org/articles/84/i34/Life-Zocor.html.

13. Jarvis, "Life after Zocor."

14. American Chemical Society, Presidential Green Chemistry Challenge: 2012 Greener Synthetic Pathways Award, "An Efficient Biocatalytic Process to Manufacture Simvastatin," https://www.epa.gov/greenchemistry /presidential-green-chemistry-challenge-2012-greener-synthetic-pathways -award.

15. Julie Zimmerman, "Big Issues: What Is Water Worth?" *Yale Insights*, April 9, 2019, https://insights.som.yale.edu/insights/big-issues-what-is -water-worth.

16. Zimmerman, "Big Issues."

17. Christoph Bode and Stephan Wagner, "Structural Drivers of Upstream Supply Chain Complexity and the Frequency of Supply Chain Disruptions," *Journal of Operations Management* 36 (2015): 215–28.

18. OECD, Central European Free Trade Agreement, "Trade in Intermediate Goods and International Supply Chains in CEFTA," 2013, https:// www.oecd.org/south-east-europe/programme/CEFTA%20IP6 _Trade%20in%20Intermediate_Web%20and%20Print.pdf.

19. Paul Anastas and David Hammond, *Inherent Safety at Chemical Sites: Reducing Vulnerability to Accidents and Terrorism through Green Chemistry* (New York, NY: Elsevier, 2015).

20. Office of Chemical Safety and Pollution Prevention, "Exposure and Hazard Information for Five PBT Chemicals," February 8, 2019, https://cfpub.epa .gov/si/si_public_record_report.cfm?Lab=OPPT&dirEntryID=342954.

21. Mulvihill et al., "Green Chemistry and Green Engineering."

22. Mollie Rappe, "Fertilizer of the Future," NC State University, March 30, 3030, https://cals.ncsu.edu/news/fertilizer-of-the-future/.

23. United Nations, "The 17 Goals," https://sdgs.un.org/goals.

Chapter 4

1. Eric D. Williams, Robert U. Ayres, and Miriam Heller, "The 1.7 Kilogram Microchip: Energy and Material Use in the Production of Semiconductor Devices," *Environmental Science & Technology*, 36, no. 24 (2002): 5504–5510.

Chapter 5

1. UNICEF, "7 Fast Facts about Toilets," November 19, 2018, https://www .unicef.org/stories/7-fast-facts-about-toilets#.
2. United Nations, "Global Issues: Water," n.d., https://www.un.org/en /global-issues/water#:~:text=Contaminated%20water%20and%20a%20 lack,people%20still%20practised%20open%20defecation.
3. Gates Foundation, "Global Growth and Opportunity," 2021, https:// www.gatesfoundation.org/our-work/programs/global-growth-and -opportunity/water-sanitation-and-hygiene.
4. American Chemical Society, "Green Chemistry Technologies Honored by EPA," June 7, 2019, https://www.acs.org/content/acs/en/pressroom /newsreleases/2019/june/green-chemistry-technologies-honored-by -epa.html.
5. Ellen MacArthur Foundation, *The New Plastics Economy: Rethinking the Future of Plastics*, January 16, 2016, https://www.ellenmacarthurfoundation .org/publications/the-new-plastics-economy-rethinking-the-future-of -plastics.
6. Ellen MacArthur Foundation, *New Plastics*.
7. Ellen MacArthur Foundation.
8. Leanne M. Gilbertson, Julie B. Zimmerman, Desiree L. Plata, James E. Hutchison, and Paul T. Anastas, "Designing Nanomaterials to Maximize Performance and Minimize Undesirable Implications Guided by the Principles of Green Chemistry," *Chemistry Society Reviews* (May 15, 2015): 5758–77.
9. Paul T. Anastas and Julie B. Zimmerman, 2003. "Design through the 12 Principles of Green Engineering," *Environmental Science & Technology* 37, no. 5 (2003): 94A–101A. https://doi.org/10.1021 /es032373g.
10. Paul Hawken, *Natural Capitalism: Creating the Next Industrial Revolution* (Boston: Little, Brown, and Co., 1999).

Chapter 6

1. Roya Jamarani, Hanno C. Erythropel, James A. Nicell, and Richard L. Leask, "How Green Is Your Plasticizer?" *Polymers* 10, no.8 (August 2018): 834, https://dx.doi.org/10.3390%2Fpolym10080834.

2. Océane Albert, Thomas C. Nardelli, Barbara F. Hales, and Bernard Robaire, "Identifying Greener and Safer Plasticizers: A 4-Step Approach," *Toxicological Sciences* 161, no. 2 (February 2018): 266–75, http://dx.doi.org/10.1093/toxsci/kfx156.

3. Albert et al., "Identifying."

4. Matthew J. Eckelman and Jodi Sherman, "Environmental Impacts of the U.S. Health Care System and Effects on Public Health," *PloS ONE* 11, no. 6 (2016): e0157014. https://doi.org/10.1371/journal.pone.0157014.

5. Eckelman and Sherman, "Environmental Impacts."

6. Andrea J. MacNeill, Harriet Hopf, Aman Khanuja, Saed Alizamir, Melissa Bilec, Matthew J. Eckelman, Lyndon Hernandez, Forbes McGain, Kari Simonsen, Cassandra Thiel, Steven Young, Robert Lagasse, and Jodi D. Sherman, "Transforming the Medical Device Industry: Roadmap to a Circular Economy," *Health Affairs* 39, no. 12 (2020): 2088–97; Martin Hensher and Forbes McGain, "Health Care Sustainability Metrics: Building a Safer, Low-Carbon Health System," *Health Affairs* 39, no 12 (2020): 2080–87; Lisa WM Leung, Banu Evranos, Alexander Grimster, Anthony Li, Mark Norman, Abhay Bajpai, Zia Zuberi, Manav Sohal, and Mark M. Gallagher, "Remanufactured Circular Mapping Catheters: Safety, Effectiveness and Cost," *Journal of Interventional Cardiac Electrophysiology* 56, no. 2 (2019): 205–11.

7. Andrea J. MacNeill, Harriet Hopf, Aman Khanuja, Saed Alizamir, Melissa Bilec, Matthew J. Eckelman, Lyndon Hernandez, et al., "Transforming the Medical Device Industry: Road Map to a Circular Economy," *Health Affairs* 39, no. 12 (December 2020): 2088–97.

8. MacNeill et al., "Transforming."

9. MacNeill et al.

10. Paint & Coatings Industry, "Anticorrosion Coating Industry Transitioning to Sustainable Development: Legislation, Intellectual Property and Industry Analysis," March 9, 2017, https://www.pcimag.com/articles/103192-anticorrosion-coating-industry-transitioning-to-sustainable-development.

Chapter 7

1. Qingshi Tu, Matthew Eckelman, and Julie Zimmerman, "Meta-Analysis and Inventory Harmonization of Life Cycle Assessment Studies for Algal Biofuels," *Environmental Science & Technology* 51, no. 17 (July 17, 2017): 9419–32, https://doi.org/10.1021/acs.est.7b01049.

2. American Chemical Society, "Toward a More Economical Process for Making Biodiesel Fuel from Algae," news release, June 18, 2012, https://www.acs.org/content/acs/en/pressroom/newsreleases/2012/june/toward-a-more-economical-process-for-making-biodiesel-fuel-from-algae.html.

3. Leigh Krietsch Boerner, "Industrial Ammonia Production Emits More CO_2 Than Any Other Chemical-Making Reaction. Chemists Want to Change That," *Chemistry and Engineering News*, June 15, 2019, https://cen.acs.org/environment/green-chemistry/Industrial-ammonia-production-emits-CO2/97/i24.

4. United Nations, "UN, Partners Warn 108 Million People Face Severe Food Insecurity Worldwide," UN News, March 31, 2017, https://news.un.org/en/story/2017/03/554472-un-partners-warn-108-million-people-face-severe-food-insecurity-worldwide.

5. United Nations, "UN Food Agency Urges Companies and Organizations to Join Global Food Waste Initiative," UN News, https://news.un.org/en/story/2012/06/413052-un-food-agency-urges-companies-and-organizations-join-global-food-waste.

6. Perry L. McCarty, Jaeho Bae, and Jeonghwan Kim, "Domestic Wastewater Treatment as a Net Energy Producer—Can This Be Achieved?" *Environmental Science & Technolology* 45, no. 17 (2011): 7100–06.

7. Stefan C.H.J. Turk, Wigard P. Kloosterman, Dennis K. Ninaber, Karin P.A.M. Kolen, Julia Knutova, Erwin Suir, Martin Schürmann, Petronella C. Raemakers-Franken, Monika Müller, Stefaan M. A. de Wildeman, Leonie M. Raamsdonk, Ruud van der Pol, Liang Wu, Margarida F. Temudo, Rob A. M. van der Hoeven, Michiel Akeroyd, Roland E. van der Stoel, Henk J. Noorman, Roel A. L. Bovenberg, and Axel C. Trefzer, "Metabolic Engineering toward Sustainable Production of Nylon-6," *ACS Synthetic Biology* 5, no. 1 (2016): 65–73.

8. Simon Neumann, Lisa-Cathrin Leitner, Holger Schmalz, Seema Agarwal, and Andreas Greiner, "Unlocking the Processability and Recyclability of Biobased Poly (limonene carbonate)," *Sustainable Chemistry & Engineering* 8, no. 16 (April 7, 2020): 6442–48.

9. Neumann et al., "Unlocking."

Chapter 8

1. "IBM Study: Purpose and Provenance Drive Bigger Profits for Consumer Goods in 2020," *PRNewswire*, January 10, 2020, https://newsroom.ibm .com/2020-01-10-IBM-Study-Purpose-and-Provenance-Drive-Bigger -Profits-for-Consumer-Goods-In-2020.
2. Jeff Sonnenfeld and Daniel Esty, "An Earth Day CEO Summit Shows How Dramatically Corporate Values Have Changed," *Fortune*, April 22, 2020, https://fortune.com/2020/04/22/earth-day-sustainability-ceo-summit/.
3. Time, "25. Thin-Film Solar Panels," Best Inventions of 2008, http:// content.time.com/time/specials/packages/article/0,28804,1852747 _1854195_1854153,00.html.

Example Scorecards

1. Andrea Larson and Jeff York, "Coastwide Labs: Product and Strategy Redesign in Commercial Cleaning Products," 2008, http://dx.doi.org /10.2139/ssrn.1278410.
2. Derek Reiber and Mike Russo, "Coastwide Labs: Clean and Green" (University of Oregon Publishing, n.d.).

Recommended Reading

For additional information on the science and fundamentals of green chemistry, we recommend the following books:

Anastas, Paul T., and John Warner. *Green Chemistry: Theory and Practice*. Oxford, United Kingdom: Oxford University Press, 2000.

Anastas, Paul T., and Julie Zimmerman. *The Periodic Table of the Elements of Green and Sustainable Chemistry*. Press Zero, 2020.

The following journal article is an informative synopsis of the concepts elucidated in the preceding two books:

Martin J. Mulvihill, Evan S. Beach, Julie B. Zimmerman, and Paul T. Anastas. "Green Chemistry and Green Engineering: A Framework for Sustainable Technology Development." *Annual Review of Environmental Resources* 36 (November 2011): 271–93. https://doi.org/10.1146/annurev-environ-032009-095500.

For additional information on the Twelve Principles of Green Chemistry, we recommend the following:

Environmental Protection Agency. "Basics of Green Chemistry." Updated December 18, 2020. https://www.epa.gov/green chemistry/basics-green-chemistry.

American Chemical Society. "12 Principles of Green Chemistry." n.d. https://www.acs.org/content/acs/en/greenchemistry/principles/12-principles-of-green-chemistry.html.

For additional information on green engineering, we recommend the following:

Anastas, Paul T., and Julie Zimmerman. "Design through the 12 Principles of Green Engineering." *Environmental Science & Technology* 37, no. 5 (March 2003): 94A–101A. https://doi.org/10.1021/es032373g.

American Chemical Society. "12 Principles of Green Engineering." n.d. https://www.acs.org/content/acs/en/greenchemistry/principles/12-design-principles-of-green-engineering.html.

For information on the impact of the principles of green chemistry and green engineering on the UN Sustainable Development Goals and the EPA, we recommend the following:

Anastas, Paul T., and Julie Beth Zimmerman. "Moving from Protection to Prosperity: Evolving the U.S. Environmental Protection Agency for the Next 50 Years." *Environmental Science & Technology* 55, no. 5 (February 2021): 2779–89. https://doi.org/10.1021/acs.est.0c07287.

Anastas, Paul T., Marcelo Nolasco, Francesca Kerton, Mary Kirchhoff, Peter Licence, Thalappil Pradeep, Bala Subramaniam, and Audrey Moores. "The Power of the United Nations Sustainable Development Goals in Sustainable Chemistry and Engineering Research." *Sustainable Chemistry & Engineering* 9, no. 24 (June 2021): 8015–17. https://doi.org/10.1021/acssuschemeng.1c03762.

Anastas, Paul T., and Julie B. Zimmerman. "The United Nations Sustainability Goals: How Can Sustainable Chemistry

Contribute?" *Current Opinion in Green and Sustainable Chemistry* 13 (October 2018): 150–153. https://doi.org/10.1016/j.cogsc.2018.04.017.

For information on the Center for Green Chemistry and Green Engineering at Yale: please visit https://greenchemistry.yale.edu/.

Acknowledgments

It is said that a book is the longest expression of a human thought. While Paul Anastas and I are the official coauthors of this book, it is really the amalgamation of many creative and thoughtful individuals' relentless pursuit of elegant science to drive leading industry practices with an intention to design a better future.

Urvashi's personal acknowledgments: I love books oriented toward presenting research in a manner that is applicable to some of the most pressing problems we face economically or in society. And every time I pick up such a book, I peruse the acknowledgments. The acknowledgments section provides a peek behind the perfectly presented material. It allows you to see the author's life and journey in creating a momentous work of art.

Thank you to my husband, Mayur Vyas, who has dedicated countless hours to proofreading and editing this work, and supported my dedication to this publication by clearing weekends (and work nights), making me coffee at night, and believing in me even when I didn't. This book has been a journey. He has often, without any complaint, set aside his own commitments and worked with me to research, source, and organize the chapters of this book and the content within. This book has seen me through my MBA, a few professional roles, one pandemic, the birth of my son, and countless other meaningful moments. The contract for this book with my amazing editor, Neal at Berrett-Koehler, was signed the week I learned I was pregnant. That was also the week I was scheduled to speak at the 75th UN General Assembly. It was a big week, and I had severe nausea and some complications during my pregnancy. Mayur has, at times like this, written sections of my work, edited it, and researched it. I do not deserve him. When I didn't have the energy to create a chapter outline, he created a skeleton draft for me so as to give me a "jumping-off point," and when I met with writer's block, he ordered pizza or planned a fun evening out with friends. Or both. During my pregnancy and maternity leave, I would often work on edits over the weekend, and until the moment I went into labor, I was still thinking of new ideas and examples that would add color to the content in this book and help bring our strategies to life for change agents globally. Mayur has selflessly supported me every step of the way. I can say with confidence that this book would not exist if it were not for his unconditional love and monumental support of all my adventures and interests.

It is said that when women support women, incredible things happen. This has certainly been true in my case. I have been so fortunate for the support of my incredible mom, Kalpana Bhatnagar, and mother-in-law, Ila Vyas, who are trailblazers and entrepreneurs. My first lessons in dedication and grit came from my mother, who raised me and my rambunctious younger brothers to dream. My grandmother was a single working mother in a young, post partition India, who raised my mom and her sister to be strong, independent women. Still, growing up, my mom had limited opportunities to pursue her dreams. She ensured that that was not the case for my brothers and me. Thanks to her, we received every opportunity to pursue our goals and to succeed. My mother-in-law is an inspiring entrepreneur, who moved to Oklahoma from India, raised her kids while pursuing her certification in cosmetology, and learned English without any formal training. She is fierce. They both have taught me to be relentless and to believe that nothing is impossible. I'm grateful to my incredible family for supporting me through this years-long project. Thank you for your humor and love, Varun, Elaine, Devesh, and Radha. Thank you to Maddison Bass for her support.

Most significant, thank you to Drs. Paul Anastas and Julie Zimmerman for your mentorship and your thought leadership. There are no words to express my gratitude, and I aim to lead by example, in the same manner that you always have.

Paul's personal acknowledgments: For whatever reason, the universe has given me the gift of wonderful family, friends, and mentors who have enabled me to endure the darkness and adore the light. The source of all my daily inspiration comes from the three most precious people in my life, Julie, Kennedy, and Aquinnah. I can never express the joy you have brought into my life. I owe a debt of gratitude that I can never repay to my parents for their love.

There are a few individuals who are very important to this book's creation, and I am so grateful for their support. Our publisher, Neal, is not only a thoughtful and brilliant editor but also very passionate about sustainability. During our journey in completing this very important work, he has understood and accommodated for life events. He has facilitated impactful conversations to provide us additional perspective on this work, and provided key guidance in the evolution of the manuscript to one that speaks to the magic of green chemistry and articulates its impact in business operations. In the process of creating this work, Neal has become a close friend, and we are so grateful for his impact in the publication process. Jeevan Sivasubramaniam is an incredible editorial managing director at Berrett-Koehler; he collated actionable feedback from our reviewers, who helped us refine our message and hone each chapter so that we ultimately ended up with the book we dreamed of writing. Rob Jolles, our advisor who introduced us to Berrett-Koehler, originally made this book a reality. Thank you, Rob—you were right. One of the most significant efforts in bringing this book to life has been through the talent and rigor of our incredible developmental editor, Danielle Goodman. Danielle excels in sharpening the message of complex, highly integrated, and interdisciplinary work and expresses big ideas with ease and sophistication. She is the Olympic athlete of communication.

From both of us: Craig Venter states, "Moving forward in science is as much unwinding the distorted thinking of the past as it is putting a clearer idea on the table." This book draws on the lifetime work and achievements of my coauthor, Paul, Dr. Julie Zimmerman, and the incredible scholars and associates who have dedicated their careers to pathbreaking science with an aim to design a new reality. Scholars at the Center for Green Chemistry and Green Engineering are working to create and commercialize entirely new and disruptive scientific solutions to some of the most pressing problems faced by humanity. This book leverages and cites their insights throughout. This publication would not be possible without their relentless pursuit of perfection in science and for the planet. We are grateful to the sponsors, donors, clients, collaborators, partners, and associates of the Center for Green Chemistry and Green Engineering at Yale University for collaborating and creatively embedding leading science into existing processes to change the economic reality for future generations.

We are so deeply honored for the time and effort of the inspiring industry professionals working every day on disruptive solutions. We thank the following individuals for sharing their stories of transformation, challenge, and achievement. Even when we were unable to include their story in whole or in part, we were enriched by their perspective, and their lessons learned deepened our understanding of this subject matter. We are moved by their trust in us to convey the depth of their action and their hard-won success stories and lessons learned: We are grateful for the incredible generosity and support of Martin Lundstedt, CEO Volvo Group. We cannot thank Mark Tarpenning enough for his support of this project from inception to the finish line. Philips N.V.: Trent Gross—thank you for leading by example and action; Harald Tepper, Bob Carelli, Simon Braaksma, and Robert Metzke, your input and example for other organizations are important; thank you for incredibly important leadership in addressing the global challenge of e-waste, even as the science is still evolving. P2Science: Dr. Patrick Foley and Neil Burns; Roger McFadden, Dr. Robert Sheehan, Dr. Thomas Kwan, Dr. Jeff Thompson, Dr. Erika Schillinger, Jill Swenson, Tammie Stark, Thomas Kruse, Dr. Jodi Sherman, Dr. Robert Dubrow, Dr. Melissa Bilec, Dr. Bob Lagassee, Dr. Andrea MacNeill, Dr. Scott Sussman, Dr. Ann Kurth, Dr. Bernard Robaire, Anthony Costello, Dr. David Penchon, Dr. Harriet Hopf, Dr. Matthew Eckelman, Dr. Cassandra Thiel, Dr. Lars Thording, Dan Vulkevich, Dr. Walter Schindler, Rob Bettigole, Stephanie Benedetto, Alexander Verbeek, Dorian Baroni, Laura Calendrella, Tammy Anderson, Charlene Lake, Joyce M. Roche, Antoinette Klotsky, Christine Bader, Tim Mohin, Jessica Leung, Arthy Hartwell, Cherie Wilson, Janet Salazar, Kristina Wyatt Schillinger, Joel Tickner, and Bob Willard. We cannot thank the visionary André Thierstein Heinz enough for his leadership and impact.

In addition, we appreciate the support of the following institutions and associations for supporting our work over the years: Elm Street Ventures, Pegasus Capital Ventures, Sail Capital, EES Ventures, the US Green Building Council, the Green Electronics Council board of directors, Chemical and Engineering board of directors, the American Chemical Society, and the Sustainable Purchasing Leadership Council.

We thank the leadership of the Yale School of Management's full-time and executive MBA for executives program for their support of this publication. While there are several individuals to thank, we are especially grateful to Dr. David Bach, Dolores Grillo, Vani Nadarajah, Maria Stutsman y Marquez, Courtney Lightfoot, and Joel Getz for their unyielding support; Yale SOM's alumni relations department and its global alumni chapters with a special mention to Javier Arguello, the NY chapter and other global chapters that continue to foster meaningful engagement between Yale and our inspiring alumni; Yale School of the Environment; Yale School of Public Health; the Center for Business and Environment at Yale; Yale Climate Communications, *Yale Insights*, Yale Sustainability; the Center for Green Chemistry and Green Engineering at Yale; Yale Divinity; and the undergraduate colleges at Yale University. In particular, the thought leadership and work of professors Andrew Leiserowitz, Robert Schiller,

Julie Zimmerman, Jeff Sonnenfeld, Zoe Chance, Teresa Chahine, Nicholas Christakis, David Bach, Daniel Esty, and Todd Cort have informed our publication. Further, we thank the leadership of Brandeis University, University of Massachusetts, and Boston University.

Many friends and family members have helped improve our drafts, provided opinions, support and encouragement, and constructive feedback. We owe a debt of gratitude to them, and it would be impossible to list everyone by name. We are so very grateful.

Index

Note: Page numbers in *italics* indicate figures and tables.

About the Authors

Urvashi Bhatnagar is a healthcare executive and population health expert. Bhatnagar's expertise lies in leveraging data analytics to improve access and delivery of critical healthcare services to communities that require it the most. Bhatnagar is widely published and the lead author of publications related to healthcare and clinical sustainability to reduce the carbon footprint of healthcare organizations. She researches, teaches about, and otherwise develops strategies to improve public health widely by influencing the levers that affect overall wellness and bringing environmentally benign and nontoxic substances to market. Bhatnagar spoke at the 75th United Nations General Assembly on the power of collaboration in healthcare and sustainability.

Bhatnagar holds a doctorate in physical therapy from Boston University and a master in business administration from Yale University.

Paul Anastas is the Teresa and H. John Heinz III Professor in the Practice of Chemistry for the Environment at Yale School of the Environment.

In addition, Anastas serves as the director of the Center for Green Chemistry and Green Engineering at Yale. Anastas served as the assistant administrator for the US Environmental Protection Agency and the agency science advisor from 2009 to 2012. From 2004 to 2006, he served as director of the ACS

Green Chemistry Institute in Washington, DC. He was previously the assistant director for the environment in the White House Office of Science and Technology Policy, where he worked from 1999 to 2004. Trained as a synthetic organic chemist, Anastas received his PhD from Brandeis University and worked as an industrial consultant. He is credited with establishing the field of green chemistry during his time working for the US Environmental Protection Agency as the chief of the Industrial Chemistry Branch and as the director of the US Green Chemistry Program. Anastas has published widely on topics of science through sustainability including eleven books, such as *Benign by Design, Designing Safer Polymers, Green Engineering,* and his seminal work with coauthor John Warner, *Green Chemistry: Theory and Practice.*

In 2021, Anastas was awarded the Volvo Environment Prize, one of the most respected scientific awards in environmental sustainability, in recognition of his transformative leadership in developing and implementing novel industrial methods to reduce or eliminate waste across numerous sectors and industries.

Berrett–Koehler
Publishers

Berrett-Koehler is an independent publisher dedicated to an ambitious mission: *Connecting people and ideas to create a world that works for all.*

Our publications span many formats, including print, digital, audio, and video. We also offer online resources, training, and gatherings. And we will continue expanding our products and services to advance our mission.

We believe that the solutions to the world's problems will come from all of us, working at all levels: in our society, in our organizations, and in our own lives. Our publications and resources offer pathways to creating a more just, equitable, and sustainable society. They help people make their organizations more humane, democratic, diverse, and effective (and we don't think there's any contradiction there). And they guide people in creating positive change in their own lives and aligning their personal practices with their aspirations for a better world.

And we strive to practice what we preach through what we call "The BK Way." At the core of this approach is *stewardship,* a deep sense of responsibility to administer the company for the benefit of all of our stakeholder groups, including authors, customers, employees, investors, service providers, sales partners, and the communities and environment around us. Everything we do is built around stewardship and our other core values of *quality, partnership, inclusion,* and *sustainability.*

This is why Berrett-Koehler is the first book publishing company to be both a B Corporation (a rigorous certification) and a benefit corporation (a for-profit legal status), which together require us to adhere to the highest standards for corporate, social, and environmental performance. And it is why we have instituted many pioneering practices (which you can learn about at www.bkconnection.com), including the Berrett-Koehler Constitution, the Bill of Rights and Responsibilities for BK Authors, and our unique Author Days.

We are grateful to our readers, authors, and other friends who are supporting our mission. We ask you to share with us examples of how BK publications and resources are making a difference in your lives, organizations, and communities at www.bkconnection.com/impact.

Dear reader,

Thank you for picking up this book and welcome to the worldwide BK community! You're joining a special group of people who have come together to create positive change in their lives, organizations, and communities.

What's BK all about?

Our mission is to connect people and ideas to create a world that works for all.

Why? Our communities, organizations, and lives get bogged down by old paradigms of self-interest, exclusion, hierarchy, and privilege. But we believe that can change. That's why we seek the leading experts on these challenges—and share their actionable ideas with you.

A welcome gift

To help you get started, we'd like to offer you a **free copy** of one of our bestselling ebooks:

www.bkconnection.com/welcome

When you claim your **free ebook**, you'll also be subscribed to our blog.

Our freshest insights

Access the best new tools and ideas for leaders at all levels on our blog at ideas.bkconnection.com.

Sincerely,

Your friends at Berrett-Koehler

Certified

Corporation